AS MEDIA STUDIES:

THE ESSENTIAL REVISION GUIDE FOR AQA

Jo Barker and Peter Wall

 Routledge
Taylor & Francis Group

LONDON AND NEW YORK

First published 2006
by Routledge
2 Park Square, Milton Park, Abingdon, Oxon OX14 4RN

Simultaneously published in the USA and Canada
by Routledge
270 Madison Ave, New York, NY 10016

Routledge is an imprint of the Taylor & Francis Group, an informa business

© 2006 Jo Barker and Peter Wall

Typeset in Trade Gothic and Univers by Keystroke, Jacaranda Lodge, Wolverhampton
Printed and bound in Great Britain by Bell & Bain Ltd, Glasgow

British Library Cataloguing in Publication Data
A catalogue record for this book is available from the British Library

Library of Congress Cataloging-in-Publication-data
A catalog record for this book has been requested

ISBN10: 0–415–36569–4 (hbk)
ISBN10: 0–415–36570–8 (pbk)
ISBN10: 0–203–96977–4 (ebk)

ISBN13: 9–78–0–415–36569–7 (hbk)
ISBN13: 9–78–0–415–36570–3 (pbk)
ISBN13: 9–78–0–203–96977–9 (ebk)

CONTENTS

PART 1

INTRODUCTION

GETTING READY

WHAT KIND OF STUDENT ARE YOU?

What kind of student are you? Perhaps it would be more precise to ask what kind of Media Studies student you are, because the same person can behave very differently in classes for one subject than for another. In Media Studies there are basically two different types of student:

- passive students
- active students

Of course, these categories are not watertight and an individual student may well move between the two categories according to many factors, including the topic being studied and their own personal and emotional state. But it is worth considering these two categories to help you focus on how to get the best from your course.

The passive student

The passive student believes that the job of the teacher is to do all the work. For the passive student, turning up at every class, writing down notes and handing in home-work is all that is necessary in order to get a good grade in the exam. Passive students want to be spoonfed information that they can repeat in the exam and pick up a certificate at the end of the course. Passive students usually manage to pass exams, but rarely achieve the grade that they are capable of obtaining. This is especially true if they have a teacher who is happy to do a lot of the work for them by not only choosing the texts they should look at but teaching them how they should respond to them. The reason for this is that the passive student becomes far too heavily reliant on the teacher and never takes the opportunity to engage properly in the discipline of Media Studies. Passive students believe that the teacher knows everything you need to know in order to do well in the exam. So long as you listen and do what you are told, the teacher will provide you with the recipe for success.

The active student

Active students want to know. Active students think for themselves. Active students are fun to teach. So what is an active student?

An active student does not rely on the teacher to tell them everything they need to know to pass the exam. Active students know how to get the best from their teacher. Like passive students they listen carefully to what the teacher has to tell them and then they go and test out the ideas for themselves.

Part of the joy of being a Media Studies student is that the texts that you engage with are not only accessible, they are also enjoyable. So if you are an active student and you have been learning about a concept such as genre, you will want to go home and watch some television or go out to the cinema in order to test out the new concept you have learned.

If you are a really active student, you will jot down some ideas about how what you have seen links into the concept of genre as you have had it explained to you by the teacher. If you are a truly hyperactive student, you will want to introduce your ideas about the text into the next class you have on genre.

Active students are autonomous. They see Media Studies as a string of concepts or theories that can be applied to a whole range of texts. The autonomy bit comes in where you go out and find the texts you want to explore through these concepts of theories rather than waiting for your teacher to tell you which texts you need to look at.

It is probably quite obvious to you which sort of student we think is likely to do better in Media Studies exams. Rather less obvious perhaps is the reason why this is the case. So let's try to explain.

Media Studies is about concepts rather than knowledge. What that means is that Media Studies examiners are more interested in how you can apply what you know than in simply finding out what you know. For example you may know about semiotics, you may be able to explain some of the different theories of narrative and you may have a good sense of what is meant by the ideological function of media texts. Your Media Studies exam will not however ask you what you know about these things, at least not directly.

For example you won't get a questions that says: 'What did Roland Barthes consider to be the significance to narrative of the hermeneutic or enigma code?' Such a question would be considered not only completely unfair but quite contrary to the ethos established for examining Media Studies. Much more likely is a question that asks you about the function of enigmas in relation to film and broadcast fiction narratives. In some ways these questions amount to something very similar except that the first is asking you to write specifically about narrative theory, the second is inviting you to use narrative theory.

Both types of question assume that you know about theories of narrative; the second question, however, is asking you to show how narrative theory can be applied to specific genres or even to specific media texts. So what the latter question is in fact doing is inviting you to demonstrate that you can apply this perspective to specific texts that you have encountered. This is where being an active student comes into play. An active student, you will remember, is one who will have absorbed the theoretical concept in class, seen the teacher apply it to examples of texts and then gone out to find texts of their own to test out the concept. So, for example, the teacher will have explained how narrative uses enigmas to tease the audience in order to hook them into the narrative flow and ensure that they remain glued to the text until the outcome is revealed.

The teacher may have used examples from crime fiction texts to exemplify this idea. An episode of *The Bill* for example offers a whole range of enigmas from solving crimes to work relationships in each episode. (At this point the passive student will decide that they have done enough and if they are asked to answer a question on narrative enigmas in the exam, then crime fiction as exemplified will fit the bill, pun intended.) The active student, however, will realise that crime fiction is a fairly obvious application for this particular concept and will set out to see how well the enigma theory will work with other texts. Soap operas, sitcoms and horror movies might be three alternative areas ripe for exploration with this new tool. So the active student will go and explore them in a number of ways; firstly and most obviously by looking at examples of texts typical of these genres. If you think about it, this is a really easy thing to do, given a listings magazine and, if necessary, a trip down to Blockbuster.

The next thing that might be useful to do is to engage in some further reading on narrative theory. With luck the teacher might have given some suggestions for this further reading. If not then any introductory textbook to media theory is likely to have a chapter on narrative theory. A quick scan of the index should also tell you if there is information about enigma codes, too. How much further reading you do is up to you. Certainly your textbook will suggest some possible further reading here and you may even consider a quick search of the Web to see if there is anything immediately available.

What is described here constitutes active independent research. It is the approach that a good Media Studies student is likely to adopt. So what is good about it? Well, instead of relying on everything that the teacher has told him or her, this student has taken the idea and tried to find their own application for it. They have tested the idea against texts that they have chosen for themselves. They have looked into further reading, both to gain further clarification of the theory and to see what other theorists have made of it.

There has been a good deal of research into how people learn. One study carried out in the 1970s at the California Institute of Technology looked at how much information people had retained 48 hours after obtaining it through a range of different methods. Their results are interesting:

- Lecture 5%
- Reading 10%
- Audio-visual 20%
- Demonstration 30%
- Discussion group 50%
- Practise by doing 75%
- Teaching others 90%

If you apply these percentages to your own learning, then you are likely to take in about 5% of what your teacher tells you. If you go and find out for yourself, then this rises dramatically to 75%. If you then come back and tell other people, for example by giving a presentation to the class, you should be able to retain almost all of the information.

Of course, this may not be a wholly accurate representation of how people learn and retain information, but it does a great deal to support the argument that your own independent learning is potentially the most efficient way to prepare yourself for an exam. Relying solely on your teacher is probably the least efficient.

So how will this help in the exam? The answer is in a number of ways:

- The active student will go into the exam room with a personal and, it is to be hoped, memorable experience of this particular element of theory. This means that they are more likely to remember the ideas and the exemplification than if they had simply copied down what they had been told by the teacher. See above.

- The examples which they have chosen will be fresh and distinct from those used by other candidates. When the examiner comes to mark a pile of scripts, s/he is more likely to seek to reward the individual response than the mass-produced responses contained in all the essays containing ideas copied from the teacher.

- The student who has done their own research will be much better equipped to adapt their response to the actual demands of the question than will the student who has a prepared answer based on their teacher's notes.

- The response of the active student will be more accurate than that of the passive student. Writing down ideas that you have got second-hand from other people is always a fraught business. It is most unlikely that you will ever do so without at least some error that will betray a lack of understanding. If you have gone to the trouble of exploring ideas for yourself, then what you write down in the exam room is likely to be a lot more accurate, not to say honest, than any attempt to represent accurately what you have been told in class.

- What you write in the exam will be yours. It will be fresh, engaged, lively and interesting. Imagine the effect it will have on the examiner who has just waded through twenty or so exam scripts that have done nothing more than tediously misrepresent what the candidates have been told by their teacher.

GETTING THE BEST FROM THIS BOOK

So you have decided to read a book on revising for your AS Media Studies exams. Good. Before you go any further, it is a good idea to think why you have chosen to read this book.

There are a number of possible reasons and knowing which one is most appropriate to you may well help you get the best from this book. The worst-case scenario is that you are going into the exam room in the near future with absolutely no idea of how to tackle the exam or exams you are taking. In this case you need to read this book fast, try to act on some of the key advice we offer and hope that it is your lucky day when you come to sit down in the exam room. If this really is the case, then, despite the fact that you do not have time to play with, it might be a good idea to work out how you arrived in this mess. It may not be entirely your fault. In the end, however, you do have to take responsibility for your own life and your own future, so, by addressing the issue, it may well be you can find a way forward to ensure that you are better prepared next time.

> AS exams are available twice a year, in January and in June, although not all schools and colleges may allow you to sit them at both sessions. It may be worthwhile considering whether you should postpone taking an exam until you feel better prepared. Of course, there are a whole range of factors to take into account, so don't make a rash decision yourself, talk it through with someone you can trust such as a teacher, parent or friend.
>
> NOTE

Another reason you might be reading this book is that you are the type of student who wants to get every bit of help that you possibly can. It may be you feel that by reading this book, you will be getting some extra advice, a little bit of inside information that will give you a good chance of getting really good grades. If this describes you, then certainly the book can help you, particularly in terms of our suggestions for revision, preparation and exam techniques. Don't, however, see the book as an end in itself. There is a real danger with books of this type that students believe the book will do the work for them. This is most certainly not the case. Don't see this as some cynical crib sheet that will get you through your exam. Read the previous section again. Are you a good student? What you learn from that is that a good media student should be setting their own agenda, not relying on a textbook to do it for them. So if you bought this book expecting model answers and other such abominations, go ask the people at the bookshop for your money back.

Chances are you are reading this book but you don't actually fit into either category. If someone called you a swat you would probably be deeply offended. By the same token you will probably have tried quite hard to get to grips with Media Studies as a subject. Some areas of the specification (the current jargon for syllabus) you will feel more confident about than others. You may feel that you have got a lot out of your Media Studies course, but that you need a little bit of help putting it all together in a way that makes sense when you go into the exam room.

If this is the case, then this book can certainly help you. It cannot, as we have said before, do the work for you, though. What you must do is figure how to use the book rather than letting the book use you. Be selective in what you read and be even more selective in how you apply it. Reading every page of the book form cover to cover will almost certainly not help you. Before you even start, sit down and get yourself sorted out.

You can start by writing down the dates and names of the exams you are due to sit and then doing a simple calculation that tells you how long you have to get ready.

Next thing to do is to make some kind of realistic assessment of what you feel confident about and what you don't. Most of you will have taken a mock exam of some sort in preparing for your AS Media Studies. This is a good starting point from which to try to figure where you might need some extra help. It may be that you need to talk to your teacher about your mock to get some advice from him or her about what you need to focus on.

NOTE

LEARNING FROM YOUR MOCK

Taking a mock exam may not be your favourite pastime, but there is a lot you can learn from the outcome. On p. 22 we suggest that you undertake a SWOT analysis in order to assess your strengths and weakness. A mock exam is a potentially really useful focal point for this activity.

Your teacher will probably have set you questions from a past paper and marked them using the exam board's mark scheme. This should give you a realistic estimate of how well you might perform in the exam itself. More usefully, however, it should also show you where you have performed well and where you have performed badly.

Not only make a careful note of the actual marks you have obtained but check out any ticks or comments your teacher has written on your mock exam script. If necessary see if your teacher will spend time going through the paper with you and helping you identify your good and bad points.

From this, you should be able to identify those areas that particularly need attention. For example in your MED2 mock, you may have answered a question on Film and Broadcast Fiction especially well and done one on Documentary quite badly. Of course this doesn't mean you can forget revising on Film and Broadcast Fiction for the exam proper, but it should suggest that you look closely at what you need to do for the Documentary question.

Once you have got some sense of what you need, look carefully to see how the book might help you. We have split it into sections so it should be fairly easy to find what you want quickly. The stuff about exams itself is mostly in Parts 2 and 3, under the headings of the two AQA exams for which you are preparing: 'Reading the Media', aka MED1, and Textual Topics in Contemporary Media, aka MED2. This is where you will find direct and detailed advice about how to take a good shot at doing well in the AS exams.

There is, however, some other useful advice throughout the book and, assuming you have time, then it is a good idea to read it. The section 'What kind of student areyou' (p. 2 above) provides the key to success or failure in Media Studies exams. It is all about your own independence and confidence in making critical judgements and applying these to media texts. If you can get your head round this idea and have the confidence to apply it, you are likely to improve your potential grade quite significantly.

We have also included some suggestions about how to revise. You might find some of this is second nature to you. If so, great – skip it. If not, then open your eyes to how you can do yourself a favour simply by getting yourself organised and ready to take the exams. Remember this is your future, not someone else's. We will spare you the clichés about life not being a dress rehearsal.

It is our belief that many students simply do not understand what they are being confronted with when they sit down to take an exam. So we have decided to tell you a little bit about the process of exam setting and marking. This is the section you can most afford not to read if you are really pushed – that is why it is at the end of the Introduction (p. 31). It does, however, contain some useful information about how the exam system works which may also help you with other exams you are taking.

NOTE

Increasingly exam boards and their regulating body, the Qualifications and Curriculum Authority (QCA), talk about transparency and accountability in the exam system. This means that, far from being a system that prevents candidates from knowing how they are assessed, they are encouraged to understand fully the assessment process. You can log on to the websites of AQA and QCA and get a lot of information about the process. The AQA website, although at times quite tricky to navigate, has become much more student-friendly. It is worth paying a visit, not least for some of the tips and hints it offers students to help preparing for and taking exams. It also gives you access to the specification itself and past papers and mark schemes. Unfortunately AQA are not so enlightened as to publish future papers to help you prepare!

WHY DO WE NEED EXAMS?

During your time in the education system you will have come across a wide range of different types of examination. Indeed one criticism of education policy is that far too much assessment takes place and that the system has become obsessed with constantly testing young people rather than giving them the opportunity to learn. Whatever the truth of the matter, examinations are here to stay at least in the short term. One reason that there are so many different sorts of examinations is that each subject or area of the curriculum requires a different approach to testing what you have learned. Some examinations will rely heavily on your ability to learn facts and repeat these in the examination. Other exams will be more concerned with your ability and skills in the application of what you have learned. Media Studies examinations are on the side of the spectrum that concerns itself with the application of skills as opposed to the writing down of learned material. This quality of Media Studies examinations will have important implications for the way in which you approach both the exam itself and your preparation for it.

Before we talk in more detail about the nature of Media Studies exams, it is worth considering what are the defining characteristics of examinations in general. These can range from tests over a period of several hours undertaken over periods of several weeks, common in art and design subjects, through to short tests of an hour. So what qualities define such diverse approaches as exams? Well, here are some things they have in common:

- *Externally set*. This means that the question or task that you are asked to complete has been set by the examination board rather than by your school or teacher. What you are asked to do will be also be asked of all other candidates throughout the country, and in some cases the world, taking the same paper.

- *Externally assessed*. This means that when you have completed the exam your work is sent off to an examiner whose job it is to mark it along with the exam scripts of several hundred other candidates who have taken the exam. Where you undertake a piece of coursework, this is marked in your centre, usually by your teacher, and then the accuracy and fairness of the marking is checked externally by looking at a small sample of the work from your centre. This process is called internal assessment and the checking is called moderation.

- *Unseen*. Although there are some exceptions, exams are generally unseen, which means that you don't know what is on the exam paper until you open it in the exam room. As you will see later in the book, this does not mean you have no idea what you will be asked and using what you do know is an important factor in getting the odds of success in your favour.

■ *Time-constrained.* You have a limited period of time in which to answer the paper. This time limit can vary widely but for most Media Studies exams is in the region of an hour to two hours. Again time constraint is an important consideration in your exam performance and one we will look at in detail later in the book.

It is important to remember that the chief function of exams is to differentiate levels of achievement. Put more simply, that means to find out the difference between students who have a really good grasp of the subject and those with rather less of a grasp. It is inevitable, therefore, that some candidates will do better than others. Our aim in this book is to help you make sure that you are one of those who do well.

Bear in mind that exams are the same for everyone. It is not just you who is under pressure: everyone feels the same. This may appear some small consolation but one important difference is that, while some people let pressure get to them and destroy their chances of doing well, smart people use the pressure to help them. Try to learn to do this. A certain amount of tension and anxiety can actually help you feel sharp and alert when you go into the exam room. Try to create for yourself a frame of mind where you use the energy to focus on the task in hand. A lot of the battle is just about thinking positively and seeing exams as an opportunity rather than a threat.

So having considered the nature of exams let's return to our initial question, why do we need exams? Exams provide an external and objective assessment of the extent and depth of your learning within an area of study. Internal assessment or coursework provides a similar check but is considered by the awarding bodies to be less rigorous than externally assessed forms of testing not least because it is easier for candidates to cheat in their coursework despite the many safeguards that seek to prevent this.

All of this has important implications for how you approach taking exams. On the one hand you can see exams as something greatly to be feared, some monstrous mechanism for catching you out and exposing your deficiencies, or you can see them as an opportunity to demonstrate or even show off the skills and knowledge you have developed as part of your study of the media. Needless to say the latter approach is the one we would recommend as the road to success. Indeed one quality of Media Studies examinations is that they invite you to adopt this approach. Their intention is not to catch you out but rather to present you with an opportunity. If you approach your media exams as an opportunity then you are likely to do well. In this book we tell you some of ways in which you can prepare yourself to take advantage of the opportunity that the exams offer. What we can't do is take the exams for you. If you are to do well, then the hard work is up to you. At least with Media Studies most of this hard work is in some way enjoyable work.

PREPARING FOR EXAMS

If you are a student taking AS level Media Studies, you will most likely have taken quite a lot of exams in your school career in order to get to this stage. It is important that you use this experience to help improve your performance in the upcoming AS exams. So in this section we want you to focus on your previous experience of taking exams and see what you can learn from it.

Think back to the last set of exams that you took. This was probably GCSE, although you may have taken some AS level exams prior to your AS Media Studies. Now ask yourself the questions shown on the opposite page.

You may find it useful to share the results of this brief survey with someone you can talk to, perhaps another student, or a teacher or a relative. What you need to try to discover is the underlying factors behind your exam performance. For example, do you perform best in exams where you enjoy the subject? If so there is a simple logic here, obviously. If, however, you perform best in exams where you don't much like the subject, you need to dig further for possible reasons for this.

You also need to consider what bearing your preparation has on your achievement in the exams you have taken. It is probably worth looking at this over several exams rather than just one, as your performance in one may not be typical. What you should find is that the better your preparation, the better your result. This is, of course, not always the case. Everyone has a story of how they, or their friend, did no work for an exam and ended up with a top grade. These flukes happen, but don't forget that the person telling you this story may not wish you to know just how much they have prepared for an exam. People like to look cool and unfazed by exams, but often you will find they have been preparing quite hectically in the privacy of their own homes.

The other big question is to consider how you actually approached the exam once you were in the exam room. For example, did you answer all the questions? Did you do the questions in a special order? Were there any other factors that might have helped or hindered your efforts to get a top grade?

What exam did you perform best in?

Why was this? (Suggest reasons)

How did you prepare for this exam?

How was this different from or the same as other exams you sat at the same time?

Were you pleased or disappointed with the result?

What was the exam you performed worst in?

Why was this? (Suggest reasons)

How did you prepare for this exam?

How was this different from or the same as other exams you sat at the same time?

Were you disappointed with the result or did you expect it?

WHAT IS AS LEVEL?

AS level was introduced for all GCE exams in 2000 when the first major revision of these exams for many years took place. The idea was to broaden the curriculum for students by encouraging them to take more than the traditional three subjects in the first year of a GCE course. It also gives students an important goal at the end of the first year of their course. One issue that the introduction of AS level has raised is the precise standard of the qualification in relation to the old A level where all assessment took place at the end of a two-year course.

> **NOTE**
>
> AS has been described as the level that a student is expected to reach at the end of the first year of an A level course. It is also intended to reflect a level between GCSE and the traditional A level. More recently examining bodies have begun to talk about 'potential' as a factor in AS performance. What is being measured is the potential of students taking AS level. A question often asked is 'What can we expect of this student when s/he comes to take the A2 examination?'
>
> This has important implications for your approach to the AS exams you are taking. It emphasises even more the importance of trying to showcase your grasp of the Media Studies concepts, theories and ideas you have met in your first year of study. You need to demonstrate your potential by show-ing how well you have engaged with the subject at this initial level. If you can show sound understanding of the basic ideas that underpin the subject then you will convince the examiner that in a year's time your understand-ing will be quite sophisticated. This should have a positive impact on the marks you receive. So a good strategy is to be prepared to be adventurous with your responses. Be prepared to try out ideas and take chances in your answers. This way you will signal to the examiner that you have engaged with and are beginning to show confidence in dealing with Media Studies as a discipline.

In preparing for the AQA Media Studies qualification, you will encounter two external exams, both markedly different in their approach. MED1, Reading the Media, requires you to write about an unseen media text, while MED2, Textual Topics in Contemporary Media, requires you to write two essay answers. Despite the different approaches required by these papers, they do have quite a lot in common and to some extent require quite a similar approach on your part. Both are 'enabling' exams, in keeping with an established tradition in terms of Media Studies assessment.

What we mean by 'enabling' is that they are designed to allow the candidate to show off what they have learned rather than seeking to expose weaknesses in candidates' understanding and skills. A particularly useful way to consider the two Media Studies AS exams is to look at them in this way:

- Your media studies course should have given you a set of skills. Your job in the exams is to show what you have learned.

- In the course of your study, you have engaged with a range of media texts across different media forms. Your job in the exam is to demonstrate that you have learned to apply what you have learned to these texts and others like them.

As you should have realised, the emphasis at AS level is on textual analysis. You need to feel confident about applying this technique both to unseen texts and to texts you have prepared ready for the exam. This focus on the analysis of text has an important bearing on how you prepare for and approach the AS exams.

A very real issue for the student of Media Studies is that both the papers that you sit at AS level could be attempted by someone who had never been to a Media Studies class. The media are an important element of the culture of this country and in consequence they are something that impacts on the life of all of us. In consequence everyone is likely to have some view on the many issues raised by the media texts we are all exposed to. It is hard to travel on public transport or sit in a café without someone expressing their views on the latest reality TV show. Indeed many of the questions set on the MED2 paper might well serve as the opening gambit in a pub conversation. 'Seen anything interesting on the telly, mate?'

That does of course raise the question: why bother doing a Media Studies course if anyone can answer the questions? The answer of course is quite a simple one. Doing a media course will give you a conceptual understanding and analytical skills that an uninformed person off the street could not hope to have. It should also be a signal for you to realise that in order to do well in AS Media Studies exams you need to demonstrate to the examiner that you have indeed conceptual understanding and analytical skills and above all that you know how to apply these. The trick is to know how best to do this.

If you eavesdrop on people's conversations on public transport or in bars for example, you will find that the media offer many opportunities for discussion. References to media issues, last night's television, the latest tabloid revelations about a celebrity scandal or the battle for the number one single slot at Christmas are an important lubricant in our social interaction. Indeed a typical MED2 question might even be used as an ice breaker or chat-up line in a social situation. Similarly most members of the public could offer you a reading of any MED1 text, a magazine cover or advertisement or a film sequence for example, simply by explaining what it means to them. So how might a Media Studies examiner discriminate between such lay opinions and the responses of a student who has followed a Media Studies course? The answer to this question provides an important key to success for the student taking Media Studies exams. What examiners are most eager to find in an exam script is clear evidence that a candidate has engaged fully and effectively in a study of the media. This evidence can be demonstrated in a variety of ways, but two particular aspects of a response would be especially compelling:

■ *Conceptual understanding.* Media Studies, as you should be aware, has an important conceptual framework. This means that there is a set of ideas and theories that inform our understanding of media texts, issues and debates. These ideas are academic concepts that place a study of the media within a framework that enables an exploration of media ideas to take place with some degree of consensus between the participants in this exploration. This approach assumes for example that when we comment on a media issue we have some awareness of previous academic writing and research undertaken previously into this issue. This means that a student of media is likely to speak with significantly more authority than a lay person for the simple reason that they will have this awareness of previous study that has taken place into the topic.

■ *Media Studies as an academic discipline has its own discourse.* Discourse is itself an academic term derived from linguistics. It describes the language which a discipline uses to discuss its subject matter. So the discourse of Media studies requires you to utilise appropriately specific technical terms when you explore issues and debates within the discipline. For example, if you are travelling home on the bus you might hear someone say: 'These reality TV shows are really mind-numbing.' If their travelling companion replies: 'Yes, it is also a genre which raises a number of ideological issues', you might conclude that while the first speaker is a clued-in lay person, the second has followed some sort of Media Studies programme. The first speaker is expressing an informed viewpoint using everyday language, while the second is using a technical vocabulary expressed within the discourse of Media Studies. You may also note that the views of the second speaker seems to carry rather more weight because they are expressed in a discourse that suggests they have some knowledge and authority within the discipline.

In Parts 2 and 3 on the MED1 and MED2 exams we offer some suggestions as to how you might do this.

REVISION

You will know quite some time in advance, usually several months, when you will be taking your exams. This means that you should have ample time to prepare for them. Exam preparation means many different things but perhaps the most important is the need to revise properly. Exam revision is synonymous with late-night poring over textbooks trying to memorise key facts ready for the exam. Media Studies requires you to do little of this, you may be pleased to hear. Although there will be some element of working with textbooks, Media Studies revision should be far more focused on tuning your mind to operate in the right kind of way to perform most effectively in the AS exams.

Of course, Media Studies revision does share some key strategies with revising for other exams, so it is useful to outline some of these now before looking at the specific revision requirements of AQA AS Media Studies exams.

The key to effective revision in one word is organisation. If you do not make a serious attempt to get organised, much of your time spent on revision will be completely wasted. Organisation has to start with your notes. By the time you are reading this, it is likely that a large amount of your note-taking has already been completed. That means that you are likely to have some sorting out to do. If you have not done so already, look at your notes in detail. If your notes are handwritten into a folder, it will probably help to have a large surface area, such as the floor, to use for this purpose. Make sure you will not be disturbed while you are doing this sorting out. Notes are only useful if:

- they make sense
- you can find what you are looking for.

> Most people use written notes, either in a folder or on a computer. One thing you might like to consider is recording some of your notes on to a portable recording device. You can then listen to your notes through headphones when you get a chance and this can be an effective means of helping you remember key information.

Read through all of your notes and filter out any that don't make very much sense. Put a note on each page of these notes to remind you what the nature of the problem is – for example, poor handwriting or the fact that you did not understand the topic your notes are intended to cover. Now try to organise the rest into topic areas that you think match in some way the contents of the unit(s) for which you are revising. If you are using an A4 loose-leaf folder, coloured dividers may help you do this. Later in this chapter where we look at the two AS exams we suggest the sorts of headings that you might find it useful to use for organising your notes. Once you have undertaken this basic organisational exercise, it is time to stand back and take stock. One thing that your notes will tell you is what kind of student you are. Here are some suggested adjectives that might be used to describe different approaches to study. Where on the scale for each do you fit?

10	1
Active (see above)	Passive
Organised	Disorganised
Conscientious	Lackadaisical
Thorough	Erratic

With any luck at least some of your responses will place you to the left of the diagram – the virtuous side. If you have put yourself wholly on that side, either you are being dishonest or you need to get a life. What the list should offer you is some sense of your strengths and weaknesses. The very best of students will have weaknesses, the very worst will have some strengths.

This kind of personal audit is called in management-speak a SWOT analysis:

Strengths, Weaknesses, Opportunities and Threats

What a SWOT analysis tries to do is to help you identify how you can operate most effectively by playing to your strengths and negating as far as possible your weaknesses. So if you see yourself as an active student with a lively and independent approach to Media Studies but are hopelessly disorganised, then you need to maximise the opportunities presented by the strength you have identified and try to tackle the threat posed by the weakness of being disorganised. This might be simply a matter of teaming up with a fellow student who is organised but generally passive and seeing if you can't co-operate with one another to make the best of your skills.

With any luck your notes will be in a condition which is at least serviceable. Unless you are extremely conscientious, there are likely to be gaps. One way to plug these is to enlist the support of other students, perhaps on a swap basis for material that they might need. If all else fails and you think the material you are missing is important to your revision, you will have to get out the necessary textbooks, or visit the appropriate websites and get up to date as best you can. If after doing some chasing in books and talking to other students you still don't understand what may be an important section of your notes, then ask your teacher to help clarify it for you. It may be that you are not the only student in the class who is finding difficulty with this topic. This will give the whole class a chance to go over the area again to ensure everyone understands the key details.

TIME MANAGEMENT

This consideration of how important are the missing notes brings to the fore the issue of time management. Ideally the time you spend on any aspect of revision should be proportionate to their significance and value to the exam you are about to take. It would be foolish for example to spend hours or even days chasing information and making notes on some aspect of the course that might not be that important in the exam itself. Equally it would be suicidal not to put effort into some aspect of the course that was absolutely certain to feature as a key element of one or more papers in the exam. The art of time management is to make this kind of judgement so that you optimise your use of the available time.

An essential aspect of time management is the decision you need to take about what to revise. There is clearly an element of judgement about this, not to say that you may also wish to take something of a gamble. The extent to which you choose, or need, to gamble may well be linked to an equation which puts available time on one side and amount to cover on the other.

In most exams, it is usually possible to get away with not necessarily covering everything in the unit specification. MED2 is a good example. As you will see on p. 74, you are required to answer questions in two sections from a total of four possible sections. In such a case there is probably little point in covering all four sections and then choosing two that offer the most favourable questions in the exam itself. In fact you could argue that this is a very foolish approach as it can only dilute your potential effectiveness in the exam. Two topics prepared properly and in detail clearly offer a potentially better response than four prepared more superficially.

This is the kind of logical decision that you need to think through in order to make sure that the revision programme that your devise for yourself is as time-efficient as possible. Of course once you have made such a major decision, you need then to put further thought and planning into the more minute detail of your revision. On pp. 75–7 we take a careful look at some strategies for approaching MED2. Use these to guide you to look at how to prioritise the areas you feel are most valuable for you to revise.

Once you have got your notes in order and decided precisely what it is you need to revise, the time has come to draw up a plan. Plans of all sorts are an important means of ensuring exam success. A revision plan is designed to help you create a timetable to use to prepare yourself so that you arrive in the exam room in the peak of condition ready to put in your best performance. You will no doubt see the parallel with an athlete preparing for an important competition. Just as an athlete does not want 'to peak too soon' or to start their preparation too late, so with an exam revision timetable you need to try to pace your revision to ensure you are at your best on the day of the exam.

So what sort of plan is it you need to draw up? Well, the first decision you need to make is when to start revising. Say you decide that a month before the exam is the right length of time, then you have just over four weeks in which to get yourself prepared for the exam. Next you need to decide how much time you can afford to spend revising Media Studies given that you will also be revising topics for other subjects at the same time. It may be best to start by thinking of how many hours in each week you think you can afford for your Media Studies revision. Be realistic about this. You may have a part-time job or other demands on your time that will make it difficult to spend the time you would really like to allocate to the subject. It is also best to think in terms of hours for each week because there may be more time at weekends than during a weekday or evening. So you may feel it is easier to have a global amount of time for the week than to try to give a specific amount of time every day.

Once you know how much time you have got, you can proceed to draw up a revision plan. Let us assume that you have decided to revise 30 days before the exam and have allocated an average of one and a half hours a day for your revision. That is a total of 45 hours. Let's assume you are also taking both AS exams in one session, MED1 and MED2. You may feel that there is more to revise in MED2 than in MED1, given the different nature of the two papers. So you may decide to allocate 30 hours to MED2 and just 15 hours to MED1. Let us consider how the 30 hours on MED2 might best be used. Well, two topics, say Film and Broadcast Fiction and Documentary, implies 15 hours for each topic. The box suggests how you might wish to split up the time in revising each of these topic areas.

NOTE

Film and Broadcast Fiction:

Ten hours roughly divided between the following concepts:

Genre

Narrative

Representation

Audience

Institution

Exemplification (5 hours)

Documentary (similar breakdown)

Remember that your revision plan is just that, a plan, not a legally binding document. Although on one level it is a kind of contract with yourself to do the work you have agreed, it also needs to be flexible enough to be modified if circumstances dictate. For example, you may find that some of the topics you have chosen for revision are more straightforward and hence less time-consuming than you expected. Other areas may demand more of your time. The value of your plan is that it serves as a reminder and a guide that will help you remain on track and, it is hoped, prevent you getting distracted or drifting off at a tangent.

Once you have decided what to revise and allotted the time for revision, you need to consider how you can most effectively get on with the job.

Notice how the revision process seems to lend itself to making lists. Making lists is a good way to help get yourself organised and to rationalise what it is you have to do. It is easy to become overwhelmed by what you feel needs to be done. Writing a list is one way to bring some sense of proportion to the task ahead. It also allows you to allocate appropriate amounts of time to each of the items on the list.

One real and unsung benefit of lists is the therapeutic value of crossing off items you have dealt with. When you start making a list, however daunting, just imagine the pleasure you will get when you cross off the last few items. The pleasure can be even greater if you have promised yourself some special treat once the last item has been firmly struck through.

It is important to remember that everyone is different. Consequently there are no hard and fast rules for how best to revise. What matters most is that you find out for yourself a method of revising that is going to be the most effective. You also need to find out a method of revising that make optimal use of your precious time. Again this means getting organised. It is quite a salutary experience to make an analysis of how you spend your time over a period of a week, broken down in terms of the 168 available hours. A fairly rough breakdown will do. It can be realised in terms of activities like:

- sleeping

- working (as in paid employment)

- study (in and out of class)
- leisure activities
- travelling

One thing you will find is that there are periods of time that you simply cannot account for. Try to figure what happens to these and if they may be time you could reclaim to allocate to your revision plan.

Another point you need to consider is how you can optimise your use of time – for example, working on the train or bus or using breaks at work or school to do some reading.

Of course this leads to an important issue about finding the most helpful conditions under which to revise. Just as some people have a happy knack of being able to sleep on the proverbial clothes line, so some people seem to be able to read, write or use a computer regardless of what is going on around them. Similarly other people need to have everything just right before they can concentrate on any kind of study activity. Most people are somewhere in between, able to tolerate a limited degree of discomfort and distraction. It is worth considering where you might fit on this spectrum, not least in order to help you arrive at some recognition of the most propitious circumstances and environment for revision. For example, you might consider some of the following factors that can influence how effectively you can work:

- Noise. Just how sensitive are you to noise as a source of distraction?

- Hell is other people. How helpful do you find it to be supported by other people? Do you work best on your own or as part of a group of people revising together?

- Attention span. Different people have different attention spans. What is your optimal attention span? Do you start to flag after half an hour and need to go do something else for a short while to get your concentration and motivation back? Or can you keep going for a couple of hours especially with the promise of a reward at the end?

- Where is the best place to work to ensure you have access to everything that you need? Remember you may need to use a computer and textbooks as well as your notes.

- Can you get anything useful done in short bursts – for example, on short journeys or during breaks? It is a good idea to make sure you always have something useful to hand such as a textbook when opportunities for short bursts of revision arise.

When you have answered all of the above questions you should be in a position to determine how best to revise. Find the right location where you can work most effectively and as far as possible without distraction or temptation. If this means staying late at school or college or working in the local library, then that is a sacrifice you have to make.

Remember too that the best revision requires you to use the plan you have drawn up in order to plan revision sessions. Regular revision is far more effective for most students than erratic cramming sessions when you seek to cover everything in one marathon period of study. A short burst of focused revision is likely to help you far more, especially if you make sure that this happens at regular intervals, for example once a day or three times a week. You should certainly think about a diary or a wall planning chart as an aid to planning your revision activities.

RESOURCES

If you are doing really last-minute revision for your AS Media Studies exams, you have probably left it far too late to take advantage of the many resources that can help you do well in the exam. You might well do better to spend your time focused on the contents of this book. If, on the other hand, you are using this book as part of a planned approach to the exams, then there are a number of places that you can go to for additional support to maximise your achievement in the exams.

Firstly there is a bewildering array of textbooks designed to help you with A level Media Studies. If you have not already done so, then you should get hold of one. The sister volume to this book – P. Rayner, P. Wall and S. Kruger (2001), *AS Media Studies: The Essential Introduction* (Routledge) – is actually written to cover the content of the AQA AS Media Studies units, so that would be a good place to start. The chapter on Reading the Media covers all the concepts that you will need to use for the analysis of the unseen text in MED1. The MED2 topics are similarly well covered with case studies on News, Advertising and Horror Movies as an example of a Film and Broadcast Fiction topic. The section on realism should also help with your understanding of the Documentary topic. There are other AS textbooks that you should have a look at if you have time, although you will have to be selective in choosing the sections that will help. Have a quick check of the contents list and index to see how much of the topics you need they cover. One other book, if you have time to read more than one, that covers much of the territory is: J. Price and J. Nicholas (2003), *AS Media Studies* (Nelson Thornes).

Of course there is a vast amount of information available to help and support you on the Web. However, you really do need to be discriminating to get the best out of it. Random Web searches may simply waste you a lot of time at this stage. There are a number of schools and colleges that offer access to Media Studies sites designed to help their own students taking the AQA specification. As these tend to change, it is not possible to make specific recommendations, but it is worth spending some time seeking them out and checking to see if there is material that can help you. Of course there are a number of established sites that can be particularly helpful, such as the sites of the regulatory bodies that control the media. Certainly the OFCOM site (www.ofcom.gov.uk/), Press Complaints Commission site (www.pcc.org.uk/) and the Advertising Standards Authority (www.asa.org.uk/) are worth bearing in mind for quick reference and perhaps to stimulate some ideas for revision topics.

Similarly some of the reference sites can provide useful support. The Internet Movies Database (http://uk.imdb.com/Browse/) provides handy links to provide quickly accessed information about films, their directors and stars. Beware, though, if you are interested in film it can become addictive. TV ARK (www.tvark.org.uk/) provides a comprehensive back catalogue of clips from television programmes that may provide interesting background material to Broadcast Fiction, Documentary and Advertising.

Don't forget though not to get yourself drowned in resources. The very best resource is your own independent thinking. Once you feel you have a good grasp of the key concepts, then go into the world of the media and use this toolkit to figure out how texts work. There can be no better preparation for either of the two AS exams.

Increasingly the Awarding Bodies and QCA itself are facing up to their responsibilities and providing support for candidates via their website. You can if you wish get in touch with the 'Exams Doctor' at QCA if you feel that you are in need of support. 'Dr A Level' smiles benignly from his home page at http://www.qca.org.uk/11449.html and even invites you to e-mail him with any queries you may have.

Similarly the BBC's guide H2G2 to Life, the Universe and Everything has some suggestions for revision and taking exams. You need to follow the links from http://www.bbc.co.uk/dna/h2g2/C521. The BBC Radio One website has some links to exam issues including advice on dealing with stress. The links are posted on: http://www.bbc.co.uk/radio1/onelife/education/index.shtml?exams#topics. Finally the AQA website has some information about preparing for and taking exams. You need to navigate from: http://www.aqa.org.uk/over/advice/index.html. You might be excused for thinking some of this stuff is a bit naff but there is probably no harm in looking.

HELP!!!!

So you have completely screwed things up. You are going into an exam tomorrow with only minimal preparation. The best you feel you can do is to write your name on the paper and leave as soon as the invigilator will let you go. Well, you don't have too much going for you. There is however a chance you can salvage something from this disaster. Firstly spend a little time figuring how this situation came about. How much of it is your fault? How much is due to circumstances over which you feel you have little or no control? OK, so there is little you can do about it now, but at least you can make sure you are forearmed and better prepared next time.

Next thing is to make a fast audit of what you do know. If you are taking MED1, then make a list of the key concepts (see p. 43) and try to write a brief summary next to each of some of the key bits of information you need to be able use in the exam. You should know by now, or at least your teacher should, whether it is a moving image or print text that you are going to be confronted with. So if it is a moving image you might like to write down:

> **Media Language: type of shot, type of edit, narrative, genre, etc.**

Do the same for all the other key concepts, especially the four important ones.

If you have time, have a quick practice run on something like a film trailer or an television advertisement which you have recorded and just try to get down some notes under the key concepts.

Finally learn some terminology. You should have some from the way in which you will want to describe shots and edits in the sequence. Learn some semiotic terms too. Denotation and connotation are a couple to get you started.

If all else fails, remember that unless you are a serial screwer-up of exams, there will be another chance in a few months' time and perhaps you will have sorted yourself out and feel better prepared next time.

If you are taking MED2 tomorrow, then you have rather a bigger problem. Busking it on the day is going to be a lot more difficult than it is with MED1. The reason for this is that you need to have something prepared to take into the exam in your head. Specifically you need some good examples of texts that you can use to exemplify some of the conceptual issues that the exam may focus on. The one thing that you have going for you, however, is potentially a really big advantage. The MED2 exam demands an engagement for the most part with contemporary texts. If you need to sort these out the night before the exam, that is about as contemporary as you can get. So this is how you might go about trying to salvage something from MED2.

Firstly check out what you know. Presumably you have been to some classes and have some notes and perhaps have read some buts of textbooks. Try to make some headings around what you know. For example you might use the key concepts yet again as headings for this. The other key issue is what two topics you are going to write about. If you go to p. 74 you will see that there is a choice of four topics. It is best to try to prepare two that have been covered in class. Of course, if you didn't actually make it to any classes and your teacher has been kind enough or daft enough to let you take the exam, then you may as well just look at any two topics that take your fancy. Cynically, Film and Broadcast Fiction and British Newspapers probably offer you the best bet.

Once you have your topics sorted out, you need to find some texts to use to support your answers in the exam. Clearly if you are looking at the two topics above, you might well use a couple of fictional programmes from tonight's television or go down to your local rental shop and get a couple of recently released titles. Similarly you can get copies of a couple of recent newspapers, perhaps using your fish and chip wrapper or the lining of the dog's bed.

A couple of hours of study on each with close application of the key concepts and you should be able to pop into the exam tomorrow and crack a decent grade! Well probably not, but if the wind is in the right direction and your good luck charms all work, you might just pass.

Of course, you will have realised by this point that it would be better to have prepared properly and not put yourself under all this pressure. So it goes.

THE EXAM SYSTEM EXPLAINED

EXAMS

The first time you set eyes on your exam paper is when it is handed to you when you are sitting in the exam room. You might like to think about how the exam paper came to land on your desk. You might also like to think about what happens to your answers when you finally hand in your exam booklet when the invigilator calls time. In this section we try to give you some insight into both the process of setting exams and the process of marking them. The more you understand the process the better you should feel equipped to handle the challenge that exams present.

Exam papers are set by a Principal Examiner. S/he is usually, although not always, a practising teacher with expertise in the subject. It is the Principal Examiner's job to prepare an initial draft of the examination paper, often as much as 18 months before the paper is to be taken. The Principal Examiner has to set a paper which reflects the demands of the unit which is being examined. If you want to know exactly what the requirements of an individual unit are, then you can look in the specification (always available on line) to check this. The PE must produce a paper that is limited to the topics in the specification. S/he must not ask questions that are outside the scope of what is written in the specification. You can see from this that the specification provides you with a useful guide to exactly what you need to know in order to pass the exam.

In setting the paper the PE must also bear in mind what questions have been set on past papers. S/he must perform a balancing act which makes sure that the paper is in line with those of previous series but is itself a new and different paper. There is also an onus on the PE to ensure that, over a period of time, all the topics set out in the specification are covered. Of course, second guessing what is going to be on a paper is a dangerous game, but it is worth bearing in mind that, if a topic has not appeared for a few series, it might well be due.

Once the PE has completed a draft of the paper complete with a mark scheme (more on this later), it is sent off to a person called the Reviser. The Reviser is another senior examiner, again usually a practising teacher with subject expertise. The Reviser's job is to consider the paper to ensure that it is accessible to candidates, that it is fair and that it reflects the demands of the specification. This means that all the questions on the paper must relate closely to what is in the specification. The Reviser may suggest changes to the paper, from just the wording of a question through to replacing one or more questions that may be considered inappropriate. An exam paper usually results from extensive discussion or even argument between the PE and the Reviser.

This, however, is not the end of the process – far from it. The papers agreed by the PE and the Reviser are now produced in the same format in which they will appear on your desk in the exam room. Prior to this they have merely been produced as drafts. The next stage is for the papers to be taken to a Question Paper Evaluation Committee or QPEC. The QPEC consists of a Chair of Examiners, the Principal Examiners and Revisers of papers which are being considered, a Subject Adviser, usually another practising subject specialist teacher, as well as the Subject Officer from the exam board, who looks after the administration of Media Studies for AQA. The job of these people is to look carefully at the paper again and to do much the same job as the Reviser did previously:

- Ensure the paper is in line with the demands of the specification.

- Make sure the questions are worded so that they are not ambiguous or confusing to candidates in any way.

- Satisfy themselves that the paper is fair to candidates at all different levels of ability.

- Consider the paper in light of those set in previous series.

- Consider the paper in light of other Media Studies papers likely to be taken by candidates during their course.

It is only after the QPEC are satisfied with the paper that it can move on to the next stage, which introduces another key player in the paper setting process – the Scrutineer. The Scrutineer's job is to act as the last line of defence in ensuring that the paper is fair, accurate and correct in all details. The Scrutineer is in fact expected to scrutinise the paper by actually sitting down and attempting it. Although this may not happen quite literally, not least because of the length of time it would take to cover all the different combinations of questions possible, the Scrutineer is expected to place himself or herself in the position of a candidate taking the paper. In doing so, it is intended that s/he will reveal any hidden flaws or problems with the paper not identified by the QPEC. The Scrutineer is also expected to check how effective the mark scheme is likely to be in light of their scrutiny of the paper and highlight any deficiencies. If this scrutiny of the paper does reveal any problems, the paper is sent back to the PE to look at again.

Assuming that everyone who has seen the paper is now satisfied, the paper now goes through a series of proof stages, again being carefully checked at each one, until it is finally ready for print and distribution to centres, where exams officers are expected to keep it under lock and key until the day of the exam.

As you will have seen, the exam setting process is a careful and deliberate one with clearly defined rules to establish the protocol for setting a paper. This is important if mistakes are to be avoided. A mistake on an exam paper can obviously have serious repercussions for candidates as well as examiners and exam boards.

One important issue from all of this is to consider what it means for you as a candidate. Well, apart from it ensuring that the paper which you receive in the exam room is as fair and error-free as possible, you might also like to think about some of the parameters by which examiners are bound when they set your paper. Notice that we identified a number of points about the paper-setting process. For candidates, the important ones of these are:

- The paper you sit must be limited to the topics in the specification. Check with your copy of the specification to be sure you know exactly what these topics are. They are given under the heading of Content for each of the AS units and consist of a series of bullet points identifying the areas that you need to cover.

- All topics in the specification should be covered over a period of time. What this means is that you can look back over the past three or four series of exam papers for a unit, most usefully MED2, and identify topics that have been popular and those that may not have appeared for a while. Of course, there would be a huge element of risk about gambling on a specific question coming up perhaps because it had not been set for a while, but you can at least look to see which bullet points in the content are popular and which are less so.

- The paper must be different from those set in previous series. Similarly it is worth looking at the most recent past paper to see what sorts of questions were set last time. Again, it would be a big gamble to assume that recent items from the content will not reappear, albeit in a slightly different guise.

■ The paper is likely, however, to follow the same style and format as those set in previous series unless the exam board had announced anything to the contrary. So for example on MED2 you can expect to have pairs of EITHER OR questions because this format has been established over a period of time.

> **NOTE**
>
> Despite the carefully orchestrated process for setting exam papers and the many safeguards that are in place, it is still possible for errors to occur on a paper. If you think there is an error on the paper or there is any unforeseen problem with the paper, alert the invigilator to this. Don't be afraid to do this, but at least make sure that you do it quietly and discreetly without alarming all the people around you. If the invigilator has to go away and make enquiries, get on with those bits of the paper that are not problematic. Whatever you do, don't just sit back and wait for an answer. The chances of a serious problem with the paper, as you can see from the information above, are pretty remote.

WHAT HAPPENS TO YOUR EXAM SCRIPT WHEN YOU HAVE FINISHED THE EXAM?

Most students breathe a great sigh of relief once they have completed their exam and then spend several weeks anxiously waiting for the result to drop through their letterbox. Few give any real thought to what goes on after the invigilator has collected their exam script. It is worth pausing for a few moments to find out about this process, not least because the insight it provides can prove useful in helping you in both preparing for and taking exams.

Each centre's exam scripts are collected by your exams' officer and sent to a designated examiner. Usually each paper is marked by a different examiner except occasionally in subjects where there are very few candidates. The examiner's job is to mark the scripts and send in the marks to the exam board, either on line or on a mark sheet which can be read by a computer. So how does an examiner arrive at a mark for your script?

Well, firstly it is important that you understand the hierarchical nature of the examination system. As you will have realised from reading the section on setting exam papers, senior examiners are generally practising teachers with a specialism in the subject they examine. This means that setting and marking exams is a part-time job for them. Exam boards employ full-time staff who are responsible for the day to day running of the exam system. Probably the most important of these is the Subject Officer, who is directly responsible for overseeing the setting and marking of exams in one or more subjects. Subject Officers are required to convene and attend all the key meetings during the year for their subject.

The setting and marking of each paper is the responsibility of a Principal Examiner. One of the PEs or Principal Moderators, who look after the coursework units, will also act as Chief Examiner, ultimately responsible for all of the units in a particular qualification.

Once the exam scripts have been collected, the Subject Officer convenes a Standardising Meeting for each unit. The purpose of this meeting is to explain the marking process to all of the examiners and to set a standard to which they are all required to mark. If the number of candidates entering for the unit is more than a couple of thousand, the standardising meeting will be preceded by a pre-standardising meeting. The reason for this is that the PE will have the support of one or more senior examiners, also known as Team Leaders. These TLs will be experienced examiners each given the job of supervising their own team of examiners. At the pre-standardising meeting, the PE and the TLs will consider a range of scripts and give each one a mark in line with the mark scheme. Ultimately it is the judgement of the PE which carries the most weight. S/he is responsible for setting the standard of the marking and in an ideal world every script that is marked will be to exactly the same standard as though the PE had marked it themselves. The standardising process then is about the PE ensuring that the marking of so-called 'assistants' is to a uniform standard set by himself or herself.

One of the many changes that have taken place in the exam system over the past ten years or so is the increased demands on exam boards for transparency. This means that the assessment system you are about to submit yourself to has to be fair and open. Transparency implies this fairness and openness by suggesting that it should be easy to see into the examining process at all stages to ensure that it is fair. Although it would be unreasonable to suggest that the system is wholly transparent, there is a lot of evidence to show that it has moved significantly in this direction. The return of marked scripts is one good example of this transparency in action. Another is the fact that mark schemes for all exams are now available on the boards' websites. Unfortunately for candidates these are mark schemes from past papers rather than the ones you will be taking, but they should still be useful to you in a number of ways.

Let us consider some of the ways in which looking at mark schemes might help you. As you will have read on p. 32, mark schemes are written by the Principal Examiner and are designed to be used by examiners to mark scripts in their allocation. Clearly one of their functions is to identify the qualities that an examiner should expect to find in scripts at the different standards of achievement attained by candidates. The mark schemes for MED1 and MED2 are divided into different levels to describe a candidate's level of achievement. The highest level is the one that you should be focused on. Ideally it describes the type of script that you are likely to produce in your examination. Even if in reality it doesn't, it should identify for you the standard of work that you should attempt to produce for each of your answers in the exam. The closer you can get to this quality of response, the higher should be your grade.

You can see an extract from the MED2 mark scheme on p. 193.

The process by which each assistant examiner is standardised is a rigorous one. At the standardising meeting itself, examiners will be expected to consider at least half a dozen scripts covering all the possible questions that candidates might have attempted form the paper. Each individual question will be marked by each examiner with careful reference to the mark scheme. The mark they arrived at will be compared to the mark given by the PE and agreed by the TLs. Where an examiner arrives at a mark different to the one agreed, his or her TL will spend time discussing how the difference may have occurred and explaining by means of the mark scheme how the PE's mark was arrived at. By the end of the standardising meeting each assistant examiner's mark should be in line with the standard set by the PE.

Of course this is not the end of the process – far from it. As soon as assistant examiners return home from the standardising meeting, they will start marking the pile of scripts they have been allocated.

NOTE

ALLOCATION

Each examiner is expected to mark around three hundred scripts for an individual unit. Some examiners mark more than one unit and some examiners mark several different units for different exam boards or in different subjects.

As soon as the assistant examiner has marked a number of scripts s/he has to send a sample of ten scripts to his/her TL for checking. This sample is expected to reflect a range of marks scored by candidates to ensure that the examiner is confident with all levels of the mark scheme, not just say the higher end or the bottom. It is the TL's job to re-mark the sample in line with the standard established by the PE.

> **NOTE**
>
> TLs have to submit themselves to exactly the same process as assistant examiners. On this occasion, the PE checks their sample to make sure that their own marking is in line with that set at the standardisation meeting. A TL cannot check another examiner's marking until the PE has confirmed that they are marking to the correct standard.

Assuming that the assistant examiner's marking is accurate i.e. in close agreement with the TL's, s/he is 'cleared' to carry on marking the rest of the scripts allocated. If the TL is not happy with the marking of the sample received, then the AE will be asked to provide an additional sample after discussing with the TL where the marking has gone wrong. If this second sample is correctly marked, then the AE is cleared to proceed with marking. If, as sometimes happens, the AE's marking is not sufficiently accurate, s/he will be asked to stop marking and return all scripts to the exam board.

As you can see this is quite a rigorous process to ensure that all examiners are marking accurately and to the established standard. If an examiner is allowed to carry on marking without having a very clear idea of the standard, then a lot of candidates can potentially get the wrong mark for their exam.

Of course this is not the end of the checking process. Other important checks are also in place:

All TLs and AEs will have further scripts checked as part of a quality control process. This is done by:

- a further sample being checked half-way through the exam process
- a review of examiners' scripts by senior examiners at the exam board office at the end of the marking process
- a statistical check to see how closely the examiner's marking is to that of other examiners by comparing statistical evidence such as the mean mark and the standard deviation.
- a check where the grade predicted by your teacher is significantly higher than the mark your script has been given.

As you can see there is a whole series of checks that take place to ensure that an examiner is marking to the proper standard. However, despite such careful checking it is still possible for things to go wrong, not least because the process relies on human beings capable of making mistakes. In the next section we look at what happens when you get your results. As you will see, this result is not necessarily the end of the process as it is still possible to ask for your script to undergo further checks.

AEs are told at the standardising meeting that they must read every script carefully in order to award marks. You can make it easier for the examiner by paying careful attention to how your script looks when it arrives on the examiner's desk. Make sure you:

- Write clearly and as legibly as possible. Having a good pen with blue or black ink will help. If your handwriting is truly awful, consider printing.
- Make it absolutely clear which question you are answering. It is a good idea to start each new question on a new page of our exam booklet.
- Clearly indicate the question by writing the number of the question, e.g. 3a, in the margin or writing out the question in full.
- Paragraph your work properly. This helps break up your answer into logical sections. A whole page of handwriting with no breaks is a daunting prospect for even the most seasoned of examiners.
- Avoid using correcting fluid (not allowed by exam boards because it sticks pages together) and pens other than blue and black.
- Use helpful signposts for the examiner, e.g. put quotes on a separate line.

Of course, even if you have written very clearly with your very best pen and followed all of the guidance above, you may still end up being disappointed with your result. On the other hand you may be very pleasantly surprised or even astounded. In the latter case you will probably decide not to get your result changed, in the former case you might. So what do you do if you think the examiners have got it wrong?

Well, all exam boards are required to provide an 'enquiries upon results' service. This means that if you think your exam paper has been marked incorrectly, there is the facility available to check it. Inevitably it is not quite as simple as that; if you appeal against your grade and you are wrong it will cost you money, about £40 in the case of a re-mark of an AS unit. There is a time limit on this as well, so you need to act quickly. The other important thing you need to know is that your school or college has to make the request for a re-mark on your behalf. They can do so only if you agree because your grades can potentially go down if the re-mark reveals you have been marked too generously.

So what is involved in a re-mark? Well yet again the AQA website provides you with useful up to date information about the procedure but there are two different types of check you can ask for. The first is a basic clerical check to make sure that the marks on your paper have been added up correctly. In the case of MED1 and MED2 this is probably a waste of time and money, given the very small number of marks to be added up. The other possibility is a full re-mark. This means that a senior examiner will be asked to re-mark your paper to check the accuracy of the original mark. Senior examiners do this fairly and objectively, seeking neither to defend the original mark nor to try to find you extra marks. They do this marking as though they were assessing your script for the first time.

> NOTE
>
> If you have a university place or job resting on the result of your AS exam, you can ask for the priority enquiries service which is a little more expensive. This means that, by your paying extra, your script will be re-marked within 20 days.

One thing you may consider doing is paying for access to your script. You can do this either as part of the enquiries service or separately. You will then receive from the exam board a photocopy of your script with all the marks and annotations that the examiner and possibly a senior examiner have written on it. This may or may not be useful to you. The real potential value of having access to your script is that you can check to see that the mark scheme has been applied fairly. It may well be that this is a bit difficult for you to do yourself, so you will probably have to enlist the help of your teacher or another Media Studies specialist, ideally someone used to marking exam scripts. What they will have to do is to do their own re-mark of the script to see if they sense that the mark you have been awarded is fair or not.

If they don't and you have had your re-mark and the exam board is adamant that it thinks your mark is fair or has even lowered it, there are still two things you can do:

- Give up.
- Ask you school to take your case to appeal.

What does an appeal involve? Basically an appeal is a two-part process. Firstly an internal investigation is set up at the exam board with an independent Scrutineer appointed to look at the issues surrounding the marking of your script. If this process fails to bring a satisfactory resolution, your school can take the case to an external appeal through the Examinations Appeals Board. Full details of the process can be found on the EAB website (http://www.theeab.org.uk/). Two things to bear in mind though are that this appeals process can take a long time and that the number of cases that actually end up at appeal are comparatively few. Most are resolved by the Awarding Bodies themselves long before this stage is reached.

PART 2

MED1 – READING THE MEDIA

INTRODUCTION

So someone has a really bright idea. They lock you in a room for an hour and a half, show you a media text and then ask you to write about it. Probably not your idea of fun. So maybe you have some right to know why you are being subjected to this. Well, here is some kind of attempt at justification.

Media texts are intended for mass consumption. They exist to be consumed. Most of the time they are consumed quickly and without very much thought. In consequence, unless they are in some way special, they don't get considered very much at all, let alone written about, except perhaps when they are selected for review in other areas of the media. The idea behind textual analysis, which is what this paper is about, is to get you to take a considered and close look at a specific media text. In doing so you are invited to bring to that text your expertise in applying the conceptual framework you have developed in studying the media.

The reason that the text is unseen is also important. On a simple level, making it unseen creates some kind of level playing field for everyone taking the exam. All candidates will start from the same position, unlike a situation where you may have been given time before the exam to prepare the text with the help of an array of friends, family and even teachers. On a more complex level, a good candidate should be able to think on their feet. If you have really taken in and understood your AS course, you should have grown proficient at analysing a whole range of different types and forms of media texts. So being confronted by one unseen in an exam should be pretty straightforward.

> **NOTE**
>
> It is worth noting that all the exam boards offering an AS qualification in Media Studies require candidates to attempt a similar type of paper in which candidates are asked to write about an unseen text. Those of you taking English Lit specifications will see readily where the idea comes from.

In the AQA specification these skills of textual analsysis are tested particularly in MED1, Reading the Media, where students have to analyse a previously unseen text in exam conditions. However, the skills employed here are also applied in using detailed textual examples in MED2, Textual Topics in Contemporary Media, and in the supporting written elements of MED3, the practical production, where you are required to analyse and evaluate a text you have produced. At A2 level these skills remain crucially important.

Therefore, it is clear that your ability to read texts effectively impacts significantly upon your success within the qualification as a whole.

PREPARING FOR AQA MED1

'Reading the Media', as MED1 is called, is a challenging, demanding exam because of the 'unseen' element and the fact that the text can be drawn from such a range of media forms and content.

Looked at from another way, however, this can be seen as an advantage because in preparing for the exam it leads you to focus exclusively on the key concepts, terminology and theoretical tools that underpin media textual analysis. Furthermore, the opportunity to deconstruct a text afresh, bringing your own individual and independent insights to bear, *should* be considered exciting, if you can approach the situation with confidence – more on this below!

THE KEY CONCEPTS

As is made clear in the specification, on the exam paper and in the marking scheme, the application of the key concepts is of prime importance to your success.

The key concepts can be listed as follows:

- Media language including Genre and Narrative

- Audience

- Representation

- Institution

- Values and ideology

Many students use mnemonics to help them to remember the names of the key concepts. Certainly you should be able to easily recall them and apply them to the given text in some detail.

There is no requirement that you cover all the key concepts in equal amounts of detail but you should probably explore Media Language, Audience and Representation in some depth to achieve even moderate success.

For higher achievement an awareness and understanding of the other key concepts is expected, though even at this level a balanced response is not a requirement.

USING THE READING TIME

Note-taking

The examination is structured to include time to 'read' and make notes about the text. Think very carefully about how you can use this time to maximum effect.

Resist the temptation to write large amounts of description of the content of the text. In the case of the print text it remains in front of you throughout so this should not be necessary. Even in the event of an audio-visual text being set, describing content is not the best use of planning time. Instead you should:

■ consider which details from the text will best enable you to explore the range of key concepts

■ record as much information as you can about these, especially details that you think you might otherwise forget once the text is no longer on view. Examples here might include:

❑ specific camera shots
❑ unusual editing transitions
❑ details of mise en scène
❑ fragments of dialogue
❑ moments when music is used to particular effect.

AND

■ think of *relevant* concepts, terminology and theories which can be applied appropriately to the text in question.

Remember though that this process of *appropriate application* is vital to the answer's relevance and effectiveness.

For example, in the June 2004 examination the set text was an excerpt from Sky News about the Iraq war. In this example a candiate noting that 'the white male news presenter is standing beside a large electronic map wearing a black suit' has made an accurate observation but such a response will not in itself accrue many marks, mainly because the approach is descriptive. The candidate has not considered the significance of what they have observed in terms of concepts, terminology and so on.

On the other hand, noting that he is 'a conventional representation of a news presenter, connoting respectability, authority and generating the mainstream audience's trust' is more mark-worthy because it does do these things. It takes an analytical, more complex approach, using subject terminology to demonstrate classroom learning.

Additionally, a strong candiate might note that 'the fact that he is standing, distantly in long shot, is quite unconventional for the news genre. This, coupled with the Computer Generated Imagery map presentation, may seek to attract a younger, more technology-friendly audience and may represent the institution of Sky as forward-thinking and modern – important values for a News channel.' Here the candidate is using their observations and conceptual and theoretical knowledge to construct a reading of the text in a sophisticated way.

- In this example note how many of the key concepts are referred to.
- Note also how developed, alternative readings are offered of a relatively short and simple fragment of text.

The reason we raise this here is to really demonstrate how important it is to think in terms of concepts and theories during the reading time and while you are planning, rather than later, almost as an afterthought.

In terms of note-taking, quality is preferable to quantity. No marks are received for the notes themselves, but the notes can often provide the basic building blocks of a good answer.

One effective strategy is to draw out a rough grid on one or two sides of the answer booklet with each box headed up with one of the key concepts. Notes are then taken in each box as you identify material relevant to each. The advantages of this are that it:

- limits the number of notes taken
- encourages you to think first and foremost in terms of coverage of the key concepts
- forms an accessible aide-memoire for you to refer back to as you write your answer in full.

Whatever the text, this opening section of the exam should be taken very seriously – you are fortunate to be given dedicated planning time in which you can

- assimilate the text's content
- deconstruct the ways in which it makes meaning

  AND

- marshal your points into some sort of meaningful order.

Planning an answer

Each point you want to make should be based on close textual reference and should draw on some area of classroom learning, probably shown by including subject terminology or theory.

Any member of the public could probably make a stab at analysing a media text – after all most such texts are offered to appeal to broad audiences. But your approach should be noticeably different from this sort of generalised, impressionistic response. What distinguishes it in the end will be evidence of classroom learning which is integrated in such a way as to develop the sophistication of your response to the text.

It is likely that you will have more points to make than time available in the exam. You should be aware of this and plan around it. At the very least you should keep a close eye on the clock and restrict the number of points you make on any one key concept to avoid running out of time with only limited, skewed coverage on a small number of key concepts.

You might want to go so far as to estimate how much you can write in a given time and plan accordingly. For example, most students, writing at speed and having completed a plan, can fill a side of A4 in about 15 minutes. On this basis you will complete four sides in an hour. How many points will this allow you to make? Using a paragraph-per-point method this should work out at around 12 major points.

This may seem a very mechanistic way to approach the exam but it can help to foreground the need to *select* from the content of the text and from the terminology and theories learnt in order to address the key concepts with some breadth, depth and organisation. The example about the news presenter and the map above shows how much meaning can be wrung from a small, simple, textual example.

ACTIVITY

Choose a print text such as a magazine cover, and make a plan of a possible answer, following the advice and guidelines above.

Ordering your ideas

Towards the end of your planning time you should look over the points you have noted and make some decisions about how you are going to order them. One senior examiner has referred to a 'golden chain' of points, one leading on logically and smoothly from another. The mark scheme makes reference to a 'well-structured' response, demonstrating 'organised understanding' – this is something to aspire to and work towards!

The most important issue here is to ensure that you are in a position to analyse the range of key concepts using detailed textual analysis. You will need to be highly selective because of the limited time available. Care must be taken therefore that your selections are judicious.

DO

- Use examples from all areas of the text.

- Choose examples of different kinds that enable you to make different points.

- Deal with key concepts in combination if you feel able to do so.

- Take charge of the response by writing about the things that you think are the most important.

DON'T

- Organise your answer by describing the text from start to finish.

- Offer lengthy denotative readings.

- Give definitions of key concepts or theories without close reference to the detail of the text.

- Concentrate on one or two key concepts to the exclusion of others.

- Offer opinions and value judgements about the text in place of analysing it.

There are no hard and fast rules about how to begin, and candidates' approaches vary, but the key is to be systematic and organised. We recommend beginning with one of the 'core' key concepts (language, audience, representation) as these are likely to be covered fully in the answer as a whole. Your choice of starting point will depend on the text you are presented with. Many good answers begin with media language and particularly locate the text's genre.

Of course you will not necessarily want to take a concept-by-concept approach, though it does have the advantage of underlining that the answer has applied the key concepts. However, the best and most confident answers are based in closely worked textual examples and consider several key concepts together, melding terminology and theory into their analysis. See p. 49 below for further discussion of this issue.

ACTIVITY

Using your plan from above, attempt to put the points into a logical, workable order – you could do this by numbering them in the order in which you will write them up. Check that you have appropriate 'coverage' across the key concepts.

In summary then, good planning involves close observation of the text, interpretation of it in relation to the range of key concepts, judicious integration of relevant terminology and theories and the organisation of an argument into a series of well-ordered points. An awful lot to do in a quarter of an hour!

WRITING YOUR RESPONSE

Starting off

Many candidates find it difficult to know how to write the opening of an answer and some fall into the trap of describing what they have seen at some length without analysing, which doesn't enable them to pick up many marks. Examiners recognise that it may take a few sentences for a candidate to 'write themselves in'.

One good way to get around this problem is just to state clearly and briefly what the text is – its form, content and perhaps institutional context. For example, in the January 2003 exam you could have begun: 'The text provided is the cover and contents pages of a computing magazine called "Computer Active".' This very simple, brief opening puts you in a position to go off in a variety of directions. You might want to:

- focus on genre, comparing it with other computing or other self-help type magazines

- make some deductions about target audience, based on frequency of issue, cover price and mode of address

- deconstruct the media language of the cover and its representations.

As you grow in confidence you may feel that you can start off in more dramatic fashion, perhaps setting up a debate from the outset and showing your personal engagement with the material. This will certainly attract the examiner's attention but be sure you know where you are going next and that you can follow up your opening assertions with supporting detailed textual reference.

Your analysis and the key concepts

The main body of your answer should consist of an analysis of the text in relation to the key concepts. You may feel more comfortable tackling these in turn, one at a time, or feel able to deal with several simultaneously.

The former approach will be well rewarded, providing your analysis is detailed and developed and a range of key concepts are covered. However, the latter approach is preferable because it is more economical and complex. In your revision try to work from the concept-by-concept method towards a more combined approach. Suppose you wrote the following:

> **America is represented as being the stronger army in the war because the newsreader tells us that the Americans now have control of the airport in Basra . . . The four and a half hour gun battle that America got drawn into is representing them as a country that never gives up and they will live to fight another day.**

A strength here is that it is clear which key concept is being dealt with – representation. There is some precise textual support but analysis of it is limited.

Or you might write along the following lines:

> **The gun battle is made more dramatic by the use of the shaky camera which produces the reality effect and is more believable to the audience. Emphasis on facts and figures portrays the event of the gun battle as heroic and honourable, and the shots of American and British soldiers fighting for their country also maintain this. The use of facts and figures represents the institution as truthful and accurate; however the use of sensationalism – 'fierce fighting under way' – and dramatisation creates an entertainment rather than informative aspect to the news coverage.**

Even if you aren't familiar with the text you should be able to see the dramatic difference in these two approaches. This example, like the first, concerns itself with representation but many other key concepts are drawn in, even if not explicitly flagged up. The effect is much more sophisticated and densely packed. Note also the sense of debate that is introduced, as though the candidate doesn't quite accept anything at face value. This is another marking descriptor for a high-level answer. (See p. 60 below).

More importantly, this second example illustrates the way in which a well-made point should be constructed. Consider using a three-part structure for each point:

- the initial assertion
- support through textual reference
- commentary that develops the point by analysing the reference.

If you are not careful, you may experience problems at any stage of this point-making process. It is important that you:

- clearly make an assertion, not taking refuge in vague waffle, not having the confidence to really make a point
- offer textual support even if you think the validity of the point is obvious so that supporting it is unnecessary, or because you find the process laborious
- offer support that is appropriate and clear.

On no account let the example speak for itself and fail to develop any commentary and analysis. Don't assume the examiner will 'work it out for themselves'!

As you can see from the example above, the development does not need to be lengthy or time-consuming, yet it can add a new layer of depth to the quality of the response.

Practise making these three-part points in relation to a text you have prepared for analysis. Try to make points that bring several key concepts into play.

COVERING THE KEY CONCEPTS IN SOME DETAIL

Media language

Candidates tend to be most confident with this key concept and write well in this area. Differentiators (the factors marking out candidates writing with different levels of effectiveness) include:

- technical knowledge and its accurate application
- analysing language features rather than describing them
- detail of response
- ability to select appropriate key details.

One way to safeguard that you are analysing in appropriate detail is to always ask questions of yourself about why a particular media language feature has been employed, or about its effects. The answer should be expressed in relation to one of the other key concepts: genre, narrative, audience, representation, institutions, values and ideology.

Each point you make should consist of a detailed reference to some aspect of the text's language, and this is likely to involve the use of media terminology or theory. In addition there will be some discussion of the significance of this feature you've observed in relation to the text as a whole and other key concepts. Don't skimp on this final element as this is where the majority of marks are picked up.

Audience

Challenges here include:

- confidently assessing audience on the basis of evidence given from the text
- ensuring these deductions are realistic and meaningful
- connecting interpretation of audience with other elements of the response.

This extract from the Examiners' Report for summer 2004 underlines some of the pitfalls candidates fall into with respect to discussing audience:

> **it was still assumed by many candidates that the audience for any media text is represented by whoever seems to appear within the text. Some candidates still try to place a media audience into some kind of age and class grouping that sometimes seems quite arbitrary, self-contradictory and stereotyped.**

You may well have been taught about various mechanisms for segmenting the target audience (t.a.) but, as the Principal Examiner's comments imply, you should use these with discretion and subtlety.

For example, decisions about t.a. based on the cost of the text are difficult to validate. If a text is 'cheap' there is not necessarily a simple correlation between this and a 'poor' t.a. A wider appreciation of social context within which the text is consumed is needed.

Deductions about t.a. and Sky subscription have caused particular problems. Candidates often deduce that because Sky is a paid-for television service, in addition to terrestrial television, the t.a. must be in socio-economic groups C1 and above, some arguing for a professional 'businessman' audience. Although on one level this is well-reasoned, the matter is more complex. Socio-economic groupings C2 and D have less money but privilege television as a key form of entertainment to a greater degree than higher-status groups. Many subscriptions are sold through mainstream sports, especially Premiership football. The mainstream, lower-class, market for Sky should not be underplayed. Bear in mind also the introduction of other satellite and cable providers, e.g. Freeview, where costs of subscription are minimised.

Beware of basing your analysis of audience on the media consumption of your own family and friends – this is not a secure basis for analysis. Rather than using textual details to make hard-and-fast decisions about the t.a. which can't really be justified, make sensible but flexible deductions – be prepared to consider several possible audience segments.

In the war on Iraq text in summer 2004 a large CGI map was displayed towards the end of the excerpt. The map filled the screen and featured simple animated graphics. Candidates who were asked to analyse this text as part of their mock exam used this information to draw rather outlandish conclusions about the t.a. such as that it was

- for the deaf
- for an unintelligent (lower-class) audience.

More sensitive readers noted:

- the unconventionality of the map in a television news context
- its connotations of a hi-tech modern approach

and concluded that the programme might be aimed at:

- a non-traditional audience not usually interested in television news
- a younger audience, based on the more modern methods of delivery.

They also noted an institutional need for Sky to compete with other news providers, therefore looking to be different in order to draw a disillusioned audience from elsewhere.

Finally, candidates used information provided about scheduling to their advantage in discussing audience:

- The Sunday morning slot might imply a family audience, explaining the accessible mode of delivery.

We cannot be sure that these readings are correct; however, they are well-reasoned, defensible and combine knowledge and understanding of several key concepts and as such are to be recommended.

Representation

Many students find representation quite a difficult concept to grasp.

Key questions to ask are:

- Who or what is being represented? How? (Language)
- By whom? (Institution)
- Who does the text suggest has power? (Ideology)
- How do the representations relate to the target audience? (Audience)
- What values are attached to the representations? (Values)

At AS level teaching and learning about representation tend to focus on categories such as gender, age, class and ethnicity.

In addition you might consider the way certain places are represented or more abstract concepts such as war, family, crime are represented in particular texts.

Of crucial importance is that you show the examiner your awareness that, whatever the representation, it cannot be fully authentic or 'real', either because of the constraints of the medium in which it is presented or because of the overriding objectives of the text, e.g. to entertain, or of the institution, e.g. to persuade.

A useful tool here is the notion of stereotyping, which can frequently be observed in media texts, though care needs to be taken in employing the term. You must consider how the person or place is being represented or stereotyped.

For example, in the television situation comedy *My Family* Michael, the younger son, is offered as a stereotypical geek or nerd – he wears glasses, reads the newspaper, has an extensive vocabulary and a dry wit, his interests are beyond his years, e.g. stocks and shares. He can be contrasted with Nick, his older brother, who is represented as a very different type of teenage male. He is of scruffy appearance, disorganised, can't hold down a job, domestically inept, interested in having sex and making money but apparently ineffective on both counts. Nick epitomises a 'live for today' attitude but his characterisation is much more complex than Michael's and the audience's affection for him as a lovable, rather feckless rogue takes him beyond the realm of a simple stereotype.

As mentioned above, places are also represented (and stereotyped) in media texts. In Richard Curtis's films such as *Four Weddings and a Funeral* and *Notting Hill* we are offered representations of London. Prominence is given to internationally recognisable landmarks, the representations appear very sanitised, with litter-free streets and high-quality attractive housing predominating. The London depicted is also strongly 'white' with other races being marginalised or absent, among both main characters and extras in street scenes etc.

Ideologically then these representations suggest that power is held by the white middle classes – a primary target audience for the films? Furthermore from an audience viewpoint, selling London to a global, especially US, audience has clearly been considered. For the British audience the sanitised 'unreal' London depicted can perhaps be seen in conjunction with the fantasy elements of the Rom-Com genre.

Another useful tool in discussing Representation alluded to in the above example is the notion of dominant, alternative and absent representations. This theory brings Representation and Ideology together and argues that certain representations predominate and consequently gain power in society. Such representations are naturalised to appear 'right' and 'true' whereas alternative representations are marginalised and their validity questioned, even to the point of their exclusion or absence.

Be aware of what sorts of representations texts are employing and why. For example, in the January 2004 exam the text set was pages from *ComputerActive* magazine, a publication whose aim is to offer plain English practical help to the less-experienced computer user. The front cover comprised a huge image of a computer screen with 'devilish' eyes peering out at the audience and a colour palette of red and black. The cover image employed represents the dangers of the internet and implies that the magazine can be used to alleviate these dangers. In so doing it feeds off a public perception of the internet as dangerous, only to represent the text itself as heroic in assuaging these fears.

Values and ideology

These key concepts, together with Institution, are often considered as a higher-order key concept and therefore perhaps of lesser importance at AS.

The specification refers to Language, Audience and Representation as the core key concepts but this is not to downgrade their importance. Indeed some very strong answers respond extensively in these areas to very good effect.

It should be clear from the comments and examples above that the Key Concepts of Values and Ideology are closely linked to Representation in particular as this is where the 'attitudes' the text is proffering are most clearly visible.

Likewise, Institution is a linked area because the 'authors' of the text can offer important clues about the text's values.

Make sure you are clear about what is meant by the terms 'values' and 'ideology'. Individual values build into ideologies which can be defined as belief systems or sets of attitudes.

Questions to ask of the text in relation to this key concept include:

- Where do you see ideology at work in the text?

- Where does the text suggest power resides? Think in terms of gender, age, class and race.

However, beware of drawing simplistic parallels between representation and power. You must carefully deconstruct the 'values' that are ascribed to a given representation.

For example, men's glossy monthly lifestyle magazines such as *GQ* and *Maxim* usually feature female celebrities on the cover dressed in lingerie and adopting sexually provocative poses. Does the fact of their prominent representation equate with ideological power? If so it is only on male terms. Their 'power' is encoded through their sexual attractiveness and nothing else. Often termed 'honeys', they are approved of as young, white, slim, buxom women. However these women are objectified in an extreme form – the male gaze is strongly implied in both the cover pose and mise en scène aspects and as such they serve to represent the ideology that women exist for the gratification of men.

In summary:

- Spend some planning time trying to identify values attached to representations within the text and how these might build into ideologies.

- Avoid making simple value judgements about texts as 'good' or 'bad'.

- Show an awareness that ideology is constructed through images as well as text (spoken or written).

Institution

When considering institution think carefully about what you already know or can deduce about the institution in question.

- Is it a capitalist, commercial organisation? (Most are!)

- Does it have a definable political standpoint? (Newspapers do!)

- Do you know anything about the personnel associated with the organisation? (Media mogul?)

- Is it a local, national, international or global institution?

- How does it make money? (Sales, advertising?)

EVIDENCING LEARNING

Most students understand that they are expected to show evidence of their class-room learning in responding to the text. What you may not be aware of is the extent to which your success in doing this is a key differentiator in terms of the marks you are awarded.

How much learning are you demonstrating?

How many theoretical terms in relation to each key concept are you familiar with? Could you use them with confidence? Your answers to these questions may provide a focus for your revision.

Concentrate on the theories you have studied and make sure you understand them well. If you want to investigate others, use the *Essential Introduction* or other books we have listed (p. 26). Some websites are also noted that may help. Unless you are confident in using the theory it is probably best avoided!

How successfully are you integrating this learning?

Is the theory or technical term you cite really relevant to this text or discussion? Are you showing that relevance clearly?

Name-dropping or feature spotting is not enough – you must use the theory to develop your reading of the text and be seen to do so in your analysis.

Likewise beware of facile, pat references to theories and concepts that don't really seem to grow from a close consideration of the text.

Students often seem to be of the view that technical terminology or reference to theory is an optional extra, the 'icing on the cake' of an answer. This is a seriously mistaken view. Your response should grow from a consideration of the text in relation to these ideas at the planning stage. In this way the theory and terminology will be embedded in your answer at every stage, not for its own sake or to impress the examiner(!) but because your interpretation is underpinned by your learning.

Examiners see a great deal of reference to theory that is undeveloped. It is as though the student considered the theory but didn't know what to do with it so they dropped it into the answer, hoped for the best and moved on. The sort of detail required is thought by many students to be 'over the top', either that or they expect the examiner to work out the significance of a theory in relation to the text for himself or herself! But that's actually your job!

Choose a text for a MED1 treatment.

Identify a theory that you think can be relevantly applied to it.

Write down how.

Then try to rewrite your application of this same theory to the text, but in greater detail.

Now introduce another, related, theory and go through the same process – hopefully this will change the discussion, moving it on and turning it into a debate!

You could write this up at speed as a 'power paragraph'.

The front pages of popular newspapers make potentially interesting texts for analysis. It is quite common to find examples of headlines which sensationalise, through either creating moral panics or adopting a xenophobic stance to issues. Typical of this was the *Sun*'s front page on 22 January 2004. The page consisted of a headline which read:

"He's a monstrosity . . . GET HIM OUT OF HERE"

This was placed alongside a close-up picture of Abu Hamza (a radical Muslim cleric) brandishing the hook he uses as a prosthetic hand. Underneath against a red background was written:

"Hook's STILL spongeing, STILL ranting . . . and he's cost YOU £1m in the last year"

We applied for permission to reproduce this *Sun* front page but News International refused. If you are intending to revise for the MED2 topic British Newspapers you might like to consider how their attitude might contribute to the debate around freedom of the press.

The extract is typical of tabloid newspapers in that it uses sensationalist language and large, dramatic full-colour images. It explicitly offers a viewpoint through both its text and its visual signs.

Relevant theory? Effects theory

How? The text is sensationalist and designed to provoke a reaction. It assumes the t.a. know who the pictured man is ('STILL') and have a negative attitude towards him ('Hook', 'monstrosity').

Greater detail? The editorial style seems to assume the readers will adopt the views espoused (hypodermic) and be likely to pass them on to others (Two Step Flow) as there is a direct call to action ('Get Him Out'). It seems likely that this could result in a reinforcement of negative stereotypical attitudes to Hamza himself and perhaps to all Muslims and British Asians, thus further suggesting that this isn't a primary target audience for the newspaper.

Second theory? Uses and gratifications

continued

Relevance? Here the audience would be considered as more active in arriving at opinions based on what they have read. Looked at in this way it might be considered that the newspaper is trying to predict the t.a.'s likely view of Hamza and to offer editorial that compliments that.

Debate? In this way the t.a. are comforted by what they read as a reinforcement of a view that they already held. So the gratification of surveillance, which one might expect a newspaper to meet is exceeded by that of personal identity and social interaction. The adoption of colloquial, familiar lexis suggests this. The redundant image of Hamza used hundreds of times in newspapers featuring his disabilities prominently and implicitly captioned 'monstrosity' underlies how unsympathetically the newspaper is expecting/encouraging the t.a. to view him.

In the box on pages 61 and 62 is a worked example of another good kind of text for analysis. The text here is an advert from *Heat* magazine for a DVD version of the feature film *King Arthur*.

Debating the point

This notion of debate is a high-level skill and is rewarded in the upper reaches of the mark scheme. It denotes a really dynamic response where the student is open to thinking about texts in alternative ways, depending on what theories or terminology are being applied. It indicates that the candidate is engaged and involved with both text and classroom learning and can 'pick up and run with' an idea.

This is a difficult skill to learn but its development will be helped if you:

- take part in debates about texts in class
- get involved with the text and develop some opinions about it
- know your theories and are able to apply them with some confidence
- stop worrying about the answer you think the examiner wants.

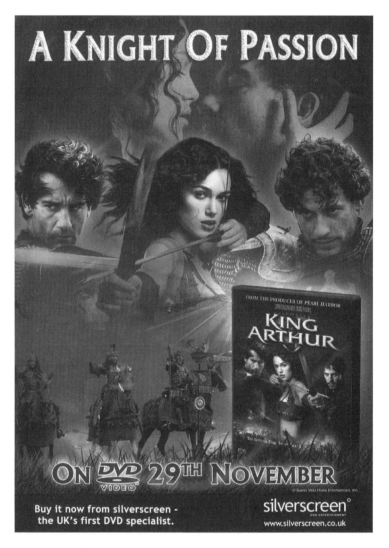

Figure 1: © Buena Vista Home Entertainment

The text features a lot of layering. Text items and the product packaging are the topmost layers, as is conventional in many print adverts. The central characters appear in long-shot in battle dress, in medium shot in action poses and close-up in a passionate embrace. These represent footage from the film itself, again typical of adverts for films, videos and DVDs.

continued

Relevant theory? Barthes's action and enigma codes

How? The t.a. are offered information – action codes – to capture their interest: for example, the battle dress and action poses suggest action sequences, high drama, period costumes and spectacular sets. This helps the audience predict the genre and content and judge the film's appeal.

Greater detail? Enigma codes are also employed to tease the t.a. to want to know more. The caption 'A Knight of Passion' is a pun. Which knight? Two are positioned in the foreground, either side of the female. This might imply they will fight over her or both be her lovers. The identity of her lover in the background is not fully clear. Some members of the t.a. may know the Arthurian legend. The battle stance of the female in the centre of the advert may present another enigma in this case, as Guinivere has not previously been presented as a warrior as she seems to be here!

Second theory? Todorov's theory of narrative equilibrium

Relevance? The theory states that narratives revolve around the establishment and disruption of equilibrium. The poster offers us three main characters occupying the central space in medium shot and full colour. Of the three the woman is the central focus because of her position and the fact that she seems to address the camera and so the audience. This suggests her importance to the narrative. We might deduce that the men either side of her will battle for her – representing conflict and therefore 'disruption'. This is reinforced by the image of a couple embracing in the background – 'resolution'? The foreground seems to suggest another narrative strand of 'disruption' with several men in battle dress facing an unseen enemy. Again this could connect with the central image where weapons of battle are also visible.

Debate? Interestingly nothing is really offered in terms of narrative resolution or closure. This can be explained by the fact that the text is an advert to buy a DVD and, like a film trailer, the outcome of the plot must remain hidden – although it is possibly predictable to the audience. The advert features in *Heat* magazine which is predominantly read by women. It is interesting to note the prominence given to the romance narrative strand through the caption, the imagery and the red wash which the whole ad is given as a successful romance is traditionally offered as a restoration of equilibrium or resolution for texts directed at women.

WHAT GOES WRONG IN MED1?

- narrow coverage of key concepts

- description rather than analysis

- lack of close reference to set text – irrelevance

- use of terminology without understanding

- generalised, unfocused analysis

- over-simplification in analysis

- lack of individual grasp or engagement with text

- use of theory misplaced.

Be aware of these common pitfalls and do all you can to avoid them. Practising the activities in this section and developing the suggested strategies should help you.

BEST PRACTICE IN MED1

- structured, organised, shaped response

- writing with confidence, grappling with the challenges posed by the text

- engagement with the text, debating its meaning – aware of and exploring alternative readings

- detailed, relevant reference to the text, ideas and theories

- clear ability to analyse and evaluate

- good understanding of the key concepts

- an autonomous answer, taking its own path through the text or analysis.

Finally, to end this section, what follows is a working through of the June 2005 MED1 paper from *J17* teenage lifestyle magazine.

Although you are not required to provide a balanced response, with reference to all the key concepts, for the purposes of the plan will deal with each key concept in turn.

2

Answer the **one** compulsory question below.

The question carries 60 marks.

QUESTION

Provide an analysis of the text: the front cover and page *three* of *J17*, published April 2004 by Emap élan Network Ltd.

- You have **15 minutes** to read and make notes on the question and the accompanying print text.

- You will then have **one hour** to write your analysis.

- You will be rewarded for making detailed references to the text.

- You should focus your analysis upon the Key Concepts of Media Language, Representation and Media Audiences.

- You may also wish to comment upon Values and Ideology and Media Institutions.

END OF QUESTION

Acknowledgement of copyright holders and publishers

J17, published April 2004 by Emap élan Network Ltd.

S301805(12)/0205/MED1

Figure 2: Reproduced by permission of the Assessment and Qualifications Alliance

Figure 2: continued

hi!

Welcome to the April issue of J17...

If there's one thing we *love* at J17, it's fashion, beauty and free stuff! OK, that's more than one thing, but a girl's allowed to be spoilt. Speaking of which, we hope you love your new glam nail kits, free with this month's issue. Which one did you choose? Our Beauty Ed, Katie's gone mad for the pink manicure set, and the Sugababes couldn't stop raving about both!

Speaking of babes, don't miss our intimate interviews with Ashton Kutcher (page 18) and new American cutie Jay Hernandez (page 50), and see what happened when our Kia got to be in the new Phixx video (page 28)! Plus we've got posters of all your favourite stars including Pink, Busted, Christina and McFly.

When we weren't busy putting together your mag, J17 hit the streets to find out all about you and your life – your style, your stories, your opinions and, of course, your boys (check out the lads in Leicester on page 57).

Remember it's your opinions that matter, so don't forget to write to us at j17@emap.com and tell us what you think of the mag.

Happy nail-painting,

Love J17

PS. Turn to page 65 for more gorgeous fashion and top tips for the perfect manicure!

email us with all your thoughts, ideas, and opinions at j17@emap.com

Heidi, Mutya and Keisha show off their babelicious J17 nail kits

"Say cheese..." J17 girls Gurj and Sarah show serious MTV presenter Dave Berry how to smile

Kia competes in the 'big Phixx hair' comp

Gurj catches up with MTV presenter Alex Zane. What a cute couple, eh?

THIS MONTH WE ♥

SPOTTY SHOES
You can never have too many shoes and these Office cuties, £64.99, come with detachable bows!

AVEDA
April is Earth month and Aveda will donate £1 to the fight against global warming from the sale of their shampoos and conditioners.

HOT CROSS BUNNY
Easter is upon us and look who popped into the J17 office!

Our fashion and beauty girls let loose in the fashion cupboard... big mistake

PHOTOS: SAM JONES, VICKI SEATON, ARCHIE WILLIAMS

Figure 2: continued

Some students respond to the pages provided in a print text one at a time but here we have amalgamated comments on the two pages to save time.

Media language

The cover offers bold colours that contrast rather than complement one another. The colours are brash and warm, especially compared to the intro page, where they are paler and more feminine. The colour palette, though restricted to an extent, doesn't communicate a sophisticated sense of design and appears rather naive.

The model addresses the camera in a medium shot with a super-smiler pose.

Sell lines are layered over her, covering all but her face. The sell lines frame her and draw our attention to her.

The text items appear in a variety of fonts, sizes and colours, and some are boxed or ringed. This variety signifies a range of content and value for money.

The use of 'screamers' – exclamation marks and question marks – signifies drama and excitement, drawing the audience in.

Repeated reference to 'you' and 'your' supports and extends this appeal for interaction on the magazine's behalf.

The intro page is offered in a letter format: 'Hi', 'love', 'P.S'. 'Snapshots' frame what little dense text there is, giving the appearance of a scrapbook or collage that may well be familiar and appeal to the target audience.

Representation

The cover model seems likely to reflect the target audience. She may represent the self as they would wish it to be, for they are likely to be younger than her. There is no hint of seduction in her pose or dress, she is a girl addressing other girls in a non-threatening yet attractive way. Her ginger hair and freckles are perhaps used as signifiers of 'the girl next door' rather than some unreachable perfection.

The dominant impression given is of sexual naivety and innocence, though there is some reference to an emerging interest in relationships and the opposite sex – 'too flirty'.

Male celebrities seem to be offered as an acceptable focus for a crush and the most risqué language is associated with Ashton (Kutcher) – 'hottest kisser', 'sexy interview'.

The voice used in the cover lines includes intertextual allusions – 'sweet dude' – and attempts to replicate the diction of its teenage target audience – 'oh my god', 'so over him'.

This is Americanised to an extent, perhaps representing the US as a desirable culture to adopt.

Audience

The primary target audience is clearly female and seems to be under the age of 17, despite the magazine's title.

There are many clues to the audience's gender, not least the nail kits and references to fashion items, including high-heeled shoes!

The innocence of the language and representations, the lack of dense text on the inner page and childish icons such as the flowers on the cover and the rabbit on the inner page lower the age range. Elsewhere a more mature approach is adopted, perhaps to broaden the audience, or to appeal to the aspirations of the younger teens.

The text content is presented in bite-size bits, and denser blocks of text are broken up with colour highlighting. All of this suggests poor concentration span or that the magazine is being consumed in short segments, perhaps collectively with friends.

The voice adopted in the copy is friendly, almost gushing, suggesting that the magazine is offering itself as a friend to the reader. Emphasis on personal appearance and grooming suggests the values of the audience are mainstream and conventionally feminine.

The relatively safe handling of potentially risky topics, e.g. relationships with boys, suggests an attempt to make parents an on-side secondary audience. An occasional nod is also given to the possible interest of teenage boys – though they are unlikely to buy the magazine, they may well read it.

Values and ideology

The overriding feeling here is that the values being offered are rather confused and contradictory.

Consumerism seems to predominate, with an emphasis on being fulfilled by buying things. Reference to 'bargains' and 'free' suggest that the target audience may be on a budget but the shoes featured on the second page seem to contradict that notion, as does the notion of a girl being 'spoilt'. In terms of relationships too the magazine seems to offer conflicting ideologies: 'single sorted' advocates self-determination and independence but 'your boys' on the second page gives prominence to the idea of relationships with the opposite sex, although it does present females as taking a proactive role within these relationships – 'check out'.

The adjectives of the intro page connote glamour and intimacy. Strong emphasis is placed on the pleasure and value of personal grooming – hair, nails – which some might argue objectifies and subjugates women.

Institution

The publisher Emap is the second largest publisher in the UK, making it a squarely mainstream publication with a strong commercial imperative. The majority of the magazine's revenue will be accrued from advertising so the editorial must toe the line in ideological terms, hence the emphasis on consumerism and beauty products. The foregrounding of free kits suggests intense competition in this saturated market segment and perhaps a flagging readership.

From notes such as these you need to develop a structured response. Note how the points can be organised in such a way that one leads naturally on to another. Indeed in places it's more meaningful to handle two or three key concepts together if you can manage it, saving time and producing a more sophisticated response.

PART 3

MED2 – TEXTUAL TOPICS IN CONTEMPORARY MEDIA

INTRODUCTION

So you have just finished writing about a text you have never seen before and all you want to do is go home and lie down, and some sadist tells you to write two essays in the next hour and half. Life is not fair is it?

Well, that is the worst-case scenario, but in today's crowded assessment environment unfortunately a typical one. Lots of you will have to take the MED2 exam, Textual Topics in Contemporary Media, straight after you have finished MED1. That means you need to be really well prepared for it, rather like a marathon runner who needs to save something for the sprint finish at the end of the race.

So what is MED2 all about? Well, one thing that should strike you as blindingly obvious is that the essay format of this paper has a lot in common with many other exams that you will have sat or be sitting. Exam questions in essay form are popular with examiners because they allow them to test a range of different skill and knowledge areas that candidates are expected to have acquired. Essays are about putting together reasoned arguments usually supported with evidence from materials that have been collected as part of your course of study. As we have already said, Media Studies exams are about learning a conceptual framework (theories) and showing you can apply them to practical situations. It follows then that a good essay on MED2 is going to be combination of these two elements:

■ a conceptual or theoretical engagement with Media Studies as a discipline

■ evidence of engagement with Media Studies texts in an analytical way that allows the application of the above.

If you can do this then you will do well in the exam. Easy isn't it?

Well maybe not, but that is the name of the game that you have to play if you are going to get a half-decent grade. Of course, as we have said, this needs a good deal of pre-planning and preparation a long time before you go into the exam room. It is no good turning up and trying to think what kind of texts you are going to use to exemplify the issues raised. These need to be at your fingertips. But herein lies one of the greatest dangers to beset the unwary candidate in the MED2 exam. You go into the exam all prepared. You have read up on the theory and got your texts ready. So keen are you to get down this information that you only take passing notice of the questions on the paper. You go in and set your own agenda, answering the question that you would have liked to appear, perhaps the one you did in your mock exam, rather than the one that is actually on the paper. If you do, then lose one grade and don't collect £200.

Directly addressing the actual question you have been set is worth an awful lot of marks. Examiners will always mark positively a candidate who makes the effort to answer the question which is set. The same cannot be said of the candidate who chooses to ignore the question.

So as soon as you get into the exam room make sure you spend a significant amount of time reading carefully the questions relating to the topics you have prepared. In fact read them until you are certain you understand exactly what you are being asked. Underline or write out if necessary key words so that you are 100 per cent sure of the questions' focus. Then and only then start thinking about how what you have prepared is going to fit into the answer you are planning.

MED2 is designed to build on your understanding of the key concepts from MED1 by inviting you to apply them to a more detailed study of selected topic areas. The specification quite clearly states what this unit is all about. The following are emphasised:

- focus on *contemporary* texts, i.e. up to date!

- emphasis on *detailed* textual study (continuing from MED1)

- *engagement* with ideas, theories and debates (a development beyond MED1)

- *evaluating* texts and ideas.

> There is a strong fixation with contemporary texts throughout the AQA specification. It is part of the effort to ensure that candidates bring their own
>
> NOTE

responses to texts rather than relying on textbook analysis of established media texts. The actual definition of 'contemporary' is, however, not entirely consistent throughout all the units. In the case of MED2 it is recommended that candidates engage with texts that are produced within the five years prior to the course. This gives you quite a lot of scope for your answers, but do be careful to ensure that you stick to this guidance. This is especially important in the Film and Broadcast Fiction section where it is easy to choose a film that appears contemporary but which was in fact released quite a long time outside of the five-year guideline. To complicate matters further, if you are tackling the Documentary section, this is one topic which does require you to have some knowledge of non-contemporary texts alongside contemporary ones.

So an additional demand here, compared to MED1, is that you show knowledge of ideas, theories and debates relevant to your topic area. This should form a key focus of your revision.

However, the ideas and theories are not an end in themselves but are used to 'enable candidates to make fuller sense of contemporary texts' (Specification 2004, p. 25). This is underlined by the weightings of the Assessment Objectives where AO3 (knowledge of theory) carries only *half* the value of AO1 (knowledge and application of key concepts). In this sense it can be seen that thorough preparation for MED1 will more than repay itself in MED2.

There are four specified topic areas, and you are required to answer one question on each of two topics. You may choose to prepare all four topics but most schools and colleges seem to teach only the two topics they expect you to answer.

Don't be tempted to tackle a question on a topic you haven't prepared, however inviting it may look! Two questions are offered on each topic area.

The pair of questions is designed to test slightly different aspects of the topic content or require you to respond in rather different ways. Look at past exam papers and mark schemes on the AQA website (www.aqa.org.uk) to glean all you can about what questions have been set previously and how these relate to the topic content, setting candidates different challenges.

When you marry up your perusal of past questions with a look at the topic content you will soon realise that there is a finite number of content areas to be tested and a limited range of ways to test them! Although there is little advantage in trying to second-guess what might come up in your exam its certainly true that 'forewarned is forearmed' in terms of being aware of what challenges you are likely to face.

No doubt by this stage in your educational career you are sick of people telling you how to do exams. You will probably be quite used to sitting exams and have honed to perfection your technique in attempting such papers. If this is the case then you can skip the next bit.

The MED2 exam lasts for one and a half hours. As we have explained, you need to answer two questions from different sections. There are four sections in total. Each section offers a choice of two questions.

The first important consideration is timing. Both the questions you attempt carry the same number of marks. One way of doing really badly on a paper like this is to spend too much time on one question and leave only enough time for an undeveloped response on the other. Two mediocre responses will generally give you a better mark than one good one and one bad one. So dividing your time appropriately is really important.

You are likely to need five minutes at the beginning of the exam to read through the paper, assimilate what is being asked of you and decide which questions you are best equipped to tackle. Similarly leaving five minutes at the end to check through your script and tidy it up is also a good idea. That leaves you with 80 minutes to do two essays, i.e. 40 minutes an essay. So make sure that you have worked out in advance when 40 minutes is up on the clock so you know it is time to move on to the second question. Make sure you don't get carried away.

The other important point to bear in mind is planning your responses. Stream of consciousness essays in which you simply pour out in random order everything that is in your head about a topic are not popular with examiners. Not only are they a pain to mark, they rarely address the question that has been set.

We spent some time looking at the idea of writing notes in MED1. Much the same applies here in MED2. If you want to write a convincing essay you need to plan it first. Don't ever just start writing. Make sure you do an outline plan in your answer book as the basis for your essay. You are expected to do this in your answer book, so take a clean page or even a double page and use it to write down all the ideas that come into your head in response to the question you have decided to tackle. Don't worry if it looks messy, this is not something that you are going to be assessed on, at least not directly. Once you have got all your ideas down onto the page, your next job is to try to piece these thoughts together into a coherent response to the question.

A good way to do this is to think in terms of paragraphs. Look at the notes you have written down and see if there are points that have an obvious link to one another. For example if you are writing an essay on sensationalism in British newspapers you might want to link an idea you have had about sensationalism to one about regulation. One way to do this is to devise a system of lettering points so that you can make these connections – thus all the points you have written down which relate to press regulation might be given the letter 'D'. Once you have finished this, you will probably find that you have half a dozen or so main points that you want to make for your essay. What you are left to do at this stage is to decide the order that you want to make the points in. Remember that a good essay will have a logical structure using each paragraph to link to the next in order to develop an idea or theme running through the essay. This idea or theme should be determined by the question you are answering.

If you use this approach to answering the questions on the MED2 paper, you will not go far wrong. Time spent in planning is time well spent, not least because the examiner who marks your script will appreciate the trouble you have taken to organise and structure your answer.

It is a good idea to spend a little time practising getting down notes and planning essays in this way. It is something you can easily do with a pen and a notebook at any spare moment you have. Simply take an essay question and write down your immediate ideas for answering it. Then try to make the connections as indicated above before coming up with a paragraph scheme for the essay itself.

Throughout our look at the topics in the MED2 exam, you will notice that we are concerned to point out to you the importance of focusing your answer on the question that is being asked. One common complaint among examiners who mark this paper is that candidates ignore the question that has been set. Going into the exam room with a pre-prepared answer is not a good idea. You need to have the flexibility to respond to one of the questions actually written on the paper. Not only does this apply to the need to focus on the specific content of the question, but you need also to follow precisely the instructions you are given. These instructions are usually implied by the verb used to tell you how to answer. Common verbs you will meet in MED2 questions are:

- Discuss

- Consider

- Analyse

- Explain

- Illustrate

You should be aware that each of these words is asking you to do something more than 'describe'. In fact if you find yourself describing anything for more than a couple of lines, then you are probably doing something wrong. Many candidates for example fall into the trap of offering plot summaries of films and documentaries or descriptions of advertising campaigns or the contents of newspapers. Words like 'discuss' and 'consider' for example are inviting you to work on a more abstract level of thinking than description. These words are asking you to engage in a debate about the issues signalled by the question. Similarly the word 'illustrate' is important. It is often used in the phrase 'illustrate your argument'. This is quite a high-level skill. What you are being asked to do is to put forward an idea and then support it with an example from a text you have studied. So for example if you write 'soap operas have turned to increasingly sensational and unrealistic story lines in order to attract and maintain audiences', then you will need to use a example to support it – for example by choosing a current story line from a soap which might be considered sensational and unrealistic.

What follows is some advice about how to prepare yourself for the exam in each of the topic areas.

FILM AND BROADCAST FICTION

This topic area on MED2 is always popular with candidates, not least because it offers the opportunity to explore a wide range of film and broadcast fiction texts. The danger, however, that you must try to avoid is that it will encourage you simply to find a few texts that you have particularly enjoyed and just go into the exam to tell the examiner all about them. This is not a good idea! By all means go find texts that you enjoy, but then you must subject them to critical scrutiny. You should do this by linking your study of the texts closely to the subject content listed in the specification and needless to say the key concepts.

So let us assume that you have found some examples of film and broadcast fiction texts that you find in some way engaging. What do you need to do in order to get yourself into shape for dealing with this section of the MED2 paper? Note that the subject content tells you to study a range of texts and goes so far as to stipulate a minimum of two for both film and broadcast fiction. You need to subject each of these texts to close critical scrutiny, which means having them available in recorded form so that you can view them on a number of occasions and also look in detail at specific aspects of the text.

The first bullet point in the specification should help get you started. It requires you to show what you know about film and moving image language and how texts are constructed. You may in fact see immediately that we are back in MED1 territory here. Yes, this is textual analysis. So this is a good point at which to jump back into Part 2 and revisit all of those techniques you learned for analysing moving-image texts. Of course you may find it easier to look at the list in the specification and make a list of the key points you need to consider. Alternatively we could do it for you:

- the analysis of image, sound and music

- mise en scène, sets and settings

- visual techniques (editing, camera positioning, lighting etc.)

- generic conventions

- non-verbal codes (basic semiotics)

- iconography.

Of course subjecting a whole film or television programme to this kind of detailed analysis may well take rather longer than you had planned. So you need to get selective in some way or other. It is always a good idea with any kind of textual analysis to find a way into the text. One suggestion is to get into the text via genre. This concept is particularly useful here because most of the texts you ate likely to consider belong to one genre or another. Putting them into a category like this should enable you to draw on your experience and knowledge of other similar texts in order to tease out some of the key textual features that are common to the genre. This might include such things as:

- character typology

- visual techniques

- mise en scène

- iconography

- use of sound

- narrative

- audience appeal

- production values

- representation.

Notice how we have immediately explored beyond the narrow confines of the text and its attendant analysis and moved into other important areas such as Narrative, Audience, Institution and Representation. It is a good idea to bear this in mind when you are making your analysis of the texts you have Chosen.

So how do you go about this analysis? Well clearly the most obvious way to get started is to watch the text right through. While you are doing so, it is worthwhile having a notebook and pen to jot down a few things:

- your immediate and first impressions of the text, particularly the pleasures it gave you

- the purpose of the text

- how you felt the text was designed to appeal to an audience

- how it is linked to similar texts you have seen

- how it was different from these texts

- how you were positioned in relation to the text

- a list of scenes that you felt were of particular interests requiring further exploration

- your evaluation of the success of the text in what it set out to do.

If you follow this list carefully you should have created a detailed summary of some of the key elements of the text. Next you need to go into more detail by picking up on those scenes you earmarked for more detailed consideration. This is where many of the items in the first point of the subject content (p. 79) should come in really handy.

So what kind of things should you be noting down? Well, start by going back to p. 44 and look at the list of items we suggested you use as an approach to the note-taking exercise for MED1. If you do this, you should certainly be covering all the items on the list above in some detail. Of course you need to do a little more than simply list what happens, but you should also seek to show you understand something of the 'why' the text is constructed in the way it is. This ties in closely to the second content bullet point in the specification, debates about meaning and evaluation. As you will have realised in looking at MED1, the issue of how texts convey meaning to audiences is a central concern of Media Studies. At the core of this is the way in which texts are constructed. The 'why' of construction should help you understand and explain the way in which the producers of a text intend it to work in communicating its meaning.

Examiners often talk about a hierarchy of skills that media students may have:

Average students can tell you 'what'.

Better students can tell you 'how'.

The best students can tell you 'why'.

NOTE

Of course you probably want to know how many scenes you need to look at for each text you choose. Well, there is no simple answer to that other than to say you need to demonstrate to the examiner that you have a detailed knowledge of how the text is constructed. This will require you to know a fair amount of the text in some detail. If you can't go into the exam and write about the how and why of the text, then you will not be able to demonstrate that you have this knowledge and understanding.

The next point in the content for this unit relates to the topic of Audience, itself a key concept. You are asked to look at

> **issues of audience, audience positioning; target audience; the text's assumptions about the audience; possible audience readings and evaluations; conditions of reception; the candidate's own reading and evaluation of the text, and the major cultural and sub-cultural influences upon this.**

So Audience, as well as being a key concept, is another area that will need your attention for this topic. You may find it useful to look at some of the strategies used to bring the text to the attention of the audience here. You can look for example at trailers for both film and television programmes to see what features of the text the producers feel are most likely to appeal to the target audience. Looking at a trailer will tell you quite a lot about some of the assumptions that a text makes about its audience through the way in which it selects specific aspects of the text and highlights or showcases these to attract the audience.

NOTE

A couple of sources that you might find useful are the British Film Institute's *Film and Television Yearbook*, published annually, and the Internet Movies Database, an on-line resource giving valuable information about cinema releases.

Audience positioning is quite a difficult concept, but one that you will find it useful to wrestle with. Audiences are positioned in a number of ways. This process is one that the audience may not always be conscious of because very often it works on a subtle level. One way into a consideration of positioning is through the representation of heroes and villains in a fictional text. Most fictional texts will have some element of conflict as central to their narrative. In any conflict the audience is generally positioned in some way to take sides. Usually this positioning places the viewer alongside the hero of the text. Look out for evidence in the text that the audience is being positioned in this way. You may find elements in:

- camera work, for example the framing of the hero and the point of view from which we are invited to view the action

- use of music to accompany characters on screen

- dialogue to influence our responses to the hero.

NOTE

How are audiences positioned in terms of gender, do you think? Do male members of the audience identify with the heroes and female members with the heroines? Is audience positioning no more complex than that? Does the idea of a hero inevitably invite our admiration?

One phrase that you might easily overlook in the bullet points refers to conditions of consumption. It might be quite an interesting way to consider how audiences respond differently to the same text. You need to consider this too, but it might be best to do so as part of your work around textual analysis where you can focus on the range of different readings that a text might offer.

Conditions of consumption in the context of film and broadcast fiction refer specifically to how and where you consume the text. Let us assume that you are considering a film that has been released cinematically. You might see the film in any one of the following contexts:

- at the cinema
- on a bootleg DVD
- on a legally purchased DVD
- on a rental DVD
- on Pay per View satellite or digital
- on terrestrial television.

You can add to this list some other variants such as:

- in the lounge with the rest of the family
- alone in my bedroom
- at a mate's house.

Notice in the first list how there is a kind of hierarchy to do with getting to see the film at an early stage in its shelf life. Think too of the cost implications of access and other issues such as screen size, sound quality and atmosphere. If you take all these factors into account, you are likely to arrive at some understanding of just how significant the conditions of consumption are likely to be on our reading of a fiction text.

We have looked above at the importance of Narrative in the understanding of how a text is constructed and how it works. Narrative can also support our understanding of other important areas. As we have suggested, narrative conflict is central to the positioning of the audience in relation to the text. Point of view is a similar narrative device which is used to position the audience. Consider in any text from whose point of view we are being invited to see the action. The answer tells you a lot about the ideological work the text is doing. Consider the following examples of fiction text genres and say from whose point of view we see the action and what impact this has on how we read the text:

- a police series
- a sitcom
- an action film
- a horror movie.

This should lead you to a consideration of identification. When an audience watches a fiction text they are inevitably inclined to identify with the characters. You may like to consider how far such a process of identification is gendered. The role of female action heroes presents an interesting potential area to explore here.

The nature of the narrative within a text is also a useful tool in looking at generic conventions. Consider for example the different types of narrative employed by different genres. This method of analysis can be applied to both film and broadcast texts. Soaps for example have their own special narrative devices in the form of cliff hangers. Very often it is the narrative outcome that tells us most about the genre. Think how different film genres resolve their narrative conflicts; how the narrative of a Western is resolved differently from that of a musical.

Representation as part of the subject content offers you a particularly broad field in which to do some investigation. Fictional texts by their very nature are concerned with Representation. They are also capable of representing a whole host of things, ideas and characters both in this world and in worlds created in the imaginations of film makers. For the purpose of preparing for the MED2 exam, it would be helpful to try to limit the extent of your exploration to something a little more finite.

To some extent the representation you look at will be determined by the texts you have chosen. For example looking at a soap such as *Coronation Street* or *EastEnders* will perhaps inevitably lead you to consider such representations as place, northern cities or the East End of London. It should also signal to you issues such as the representation of community and working-class life. Gender and age are also very much to the fore as issues in soap opera. *Coronation Street* has long been known for its strong women characters, although more recently gay characters have come to feature as a significant minority. Ethnicity and disability have also become the focus for representational issues within these serial dramas. Similarly you can choose a range of film and broadcast fiction texts that will throw up similar issues of Representation.

You can link some of these into your narrative study in the form of both character typology in the form of stereotypes and stock characters as well as the representation of heroes and villains – for example the emphasis that is generally placed on male heroes in Hollywood films and those occasions when this convention is broken and women are give the lead roles as protagonists.

The last point may well stimulate in you some ideas about the appropriateness, fairness and accuracy of the representations that you find in films and broadcast fiction. Certainly you may not only want to question the accuracy of representations created by Hollywood for example, but you might also feel that you want to investigate in whose interests any misrepresentations are made. What is the ideological work these texts are doing? A look at the ITV series *The Bill* might provide an interesting starting point.

Institution should also provide you with an interesting focus for your consideration of fictional texts. Again the subject content suggests some of the areas that you might explore.

- institutional issues (influence of film or broadcasting institutions upon texts)

- differences within film and broadcasting institutions, e.g. Hollywood versus non-Hollywood

- public service versus commercial broadcasting

- influence of finance, marketing and distribution upon the production and reception of texts

- debates around aesthetic value, profit, public-service values etc.

Many of these areas are perhaps best seen as background detail rather than being central to your study of your texts. It is important, however, that you find out something of the institutional context that produced your text. For example most films that are screened at multiplex cinemas in this country are made in Hollywood. There are, however, still films made independently of the Hollywood system. European countries such as France and Italy have well-established traditions of national cinema producing home-grown products. The origin of a film is therefore often important in terms of how it is marketed and received by audiences, as well as having crucial implications for the messages and values which it contains.

Similarly many television fiction programmes are the products of the American television industry. Some of course are home-grown. Identifying the difference between the two is important, as is being aware of the difference between BBC-produced texts and those produced by commercial television. The BBC is financed by public money which means that it is able, at least in theory, to be more adventurous in the programmes it makes than commercial channels that have to please advertisers by having large audiences.

Your exploration of this institutional context may also enable you to give consideration to the value of the texts from an aesthetic perspective. Most fiction texts are created for mass consumption and in consequence for giving audiences immediate pleasure. Others are, however, considered to be of more lasting worth.

A film such as *Citizen Kane* (1940) for example is considered to be a classic of the cinema. Although you are dealing with contemporary examples that will not yet have stood the test of time, you may also feel you can make judgements about the aesthetic value of the texts you have studied. Of course another way of looking at the success of a text is in terms of its commercial value. Box office takings are a guide to the success of a film released at the cinema while audience viewing figures are the means of measuring the popularity of a television programme. You might like to consider the relationship between commercial success and aesthetic value for the texts you have studied.

ACTIVITY

> *Consider the texts that you have studied. Write down as much information as you can about where they were produced and by what sort of organisation. Now, for each one, try to explain how you think this might have influenced the nature of the text and its appeal to the audience.*

We have mentioned above several times the idea that you should choose texts to use in the exam to support your answer. The texts you choose and the way in which you choose them are fundamental to producing a good response to this question. Remember how we talked earlier on about active and passive students? Well, this is one place where you can clearly demonstrate just how active you can be as a student. In preparing you for this exam, your teacher will have no doubt looked at with the class a series of different examples of film and broadcast fiction texts. Many of your classmates will adopt the attitude that this has done the work for them and so they will want to use these examples in the exam. If you have got any sense, you will go out and find your own examples, for all the reasons we gave you earlier (p. 3). Of course, it is a good idea to seek advice and guidance from your teacher not only about your choice of texts but also how you are going to approach them. In the end, however, this is your decision and it is a good idea to be ruled by your heart on this one, choosing either texts you love or even texts you loathe.

Don't forget that texts must be contemporary. That means produced in the past five years. The word 'produced' is also important. In this postmodern world, the repackaging of texts from producers' back catalogues is commonplace. A film re-released on DVD or a sitcom broadcast on satellite is not a contemporary text unless it was produced within the timespan indicated in the guidelines.

Don't forget you must be able to have access to the texts for detailed study. That means viewing them several times and analysing specific scenes or segments in considerable detail. Finding access to contemporary texts that will allow you to do this is something of a balancing act.

Remember that you will need to do some background research, particularly in terms of audience and institutions. When you choose the texts you want to explore, make sure that you will be able to get access to this information. You may find it useful to keep a scrapbook of information that you manage to gather.

Finally don't forget that while examiners will always be impressed by your enthusiastic response to the texts, they are looking for something more. The something more is about using the conceptual framework outlined above as a way of writing about these texts in a critical and analytical way. The texts you have chosen should be used to illustrate the points you want to make in response to the question. Don't just write about the texts because you like them or want to be the boring person who needs to tell everyone about the plot of every film they have ever seen.

You need to:

- focus on the question

- demonstrate your understanding of the concepts

- evaluate the texts within a critical framework

- show knowledge of the texts to illustrate your points.

Let's have a look at some past exam questions and think about how to tackle them.

In January 2005 question 1a reproduced a chart of the top twenty television shows for the week ending 9 November 2003 from *The Total TV Guide*. Question (1a) asked:

EXAM QUESTION

More than half of the programmes in the above chart are examples of fictional texts.

Account for the popularity of broadcast fiction with television audiences.

Support your argument with illustrations from a range of texts that you have studied.

(You may refer to any of the fictional texts in the chart or to any others you have studied.)

AQA 2005

Let's have a look at what this question is getting at before we consider the alternative question.

The focus of the question is clearly broadcast fiction texts on television, although the chart does contain one feature film shown on ITV1. In many ways the chart itself is not directly relevant to the question. It serves to act as a stimulus to get you thinking about just how popular fiction texts are on television, with *Coronation Street* at the head of the list with nearly 15 million viewers.

The crux of the question is the sentence: 'Account for the popularity of broadcast fiction with television audiences.' So the question is about how fictional texts appeal to audiences and, perhaps by implication, how they maintain that appeal.

This is a good time to write down a list of key points that you would want to include in your response if you chose to tackle this question. You might start your list by thinking about:

■ *the appeal of fictional texts*

■ *the types of audience that are targeted*

■ *the pleasures audiences might obtain from consuming fictional texts*

■ *the importance of formats and genre formulas.*

Of course your response to this question is going to be determined to some degree by the texts that you have studied. You are asked to support your answer with illustrations from a range of texts you have studied. It is going to be useful therefore if you have looked at broadcast fiction texts across several different genres, although you might argue that you could produce an effective answer based on a study of soaps.

Let's look at the alternative question from January 2005 before we come back and consider this one in more detail. Question (1b) asked:

EXAM QUESTION

Provide a detailed analysis of one film AND/OR one broadcast fictional text, explaining how the elements of its construction engage its audience.

You may wish to consider some of the following:

■ Narrative devices and structures

■ Film and broadcast fiction techniques

■ The appeal of characters or stars

■ Inclusion of themes or issues

AQA 2005

Again the question can be summed up in the first sentence. The additional material, sometimes called the scaffolding, is there to help support you by offering suggestions about what you may want to consider. Pay careful attention to the word 'may'. This is not a checklist of items you must cover. It is a list of possible options on which you might focus. If you want you can ignore it completely. The reason it is there, however, is to try to stop you falling into the trap frequented by so many students who interpret the questions as: 'Write about a film or television programme that you like. Include lots of description of the plot and characters.'

One approach to a question is to underline the key words that your answer needs to address. What four key words would you want to highlight in this question?

ACTIVITY

The words that you must take notice of are:

■ *Detailed*: as opposed to superficial so that you can show you really know the text well

■ *Analysis*: as opposed to description so that you can explain the how and why of the text

■ *Construction*: in the sense of how the text had been put together

■ *Audience*: what are the pleasures these people get from consuming this text?

So which one of this pair, (1a) or (1b), would you choose? Well, question (1a) limits you to writing about television texts, so if the entire focus of your study has been film then you really should not be trying to answer this question. Question (1b) gives you a choice of film or broadcast fiction texts so whatever you have studied for this topic should fit the bill.

What you should have spotted is that the key difference between the two questions is that (a) is a broad-based question in that it invites you to use a range of texts to account for the popularity of broadcast fiction. No precise definition of range is given but it is reasonable to assume that range certainly implies more than one and probably rather more than two. So to answer this question you need to be able to cite examples from several television fictional texts that can support your assertion about the popularity of the genre.

On the other hand question (1b) is about depth and detail. Here you are invited to look just at one or two texts. This means that if you choose to focus on just the one text you need to know that text in sufficient detail to sustain your answer over a period of 45 minutes. Even if you go for two texts you need again to have sufficient detailed knowledge to sustain your response.

> *Try putting together a very quick essay plan for each of these questions. On the basis of your plan, which do you think you are better equipped to answer?*

Let's have a look at what candidates taking the MED2 exam in June 2005 were confronted with. Here are the two questions from the Film and Broadcast Fiction section of the paper:

EXAM QUESTION

(a) Account for the similarities you have found in the techniques used to tell stories by those who make film and broadcast fiction.

Give textual illustration from film AND/OR broadcast fiction texts to support your argument.

(b) 'Film and television fiction texts are always based on contemporary issues and attitudes.'

> How far do you agree with this statement? Support your argument with a
> detailed reading of one film OR one broadcast fiction text that you know well.
> AQA 2005

Before we go any further, read them again and decide which one you think would
be the better for you to tackle. You should also try to explain why you think one would
be better than the other. Because it looks easier is not sufficient reason.

So what are the differences? Well, one important and immediate difference is that
(a) asks for a wide-ranging response across several different texts while (b) asks for
a close reading of just one text.

Note that both questions allow you to use both film and broadcast fiction as the
basis for your response so you have a lot of freedom here in deciding which of
the two questions is going to be better for you.

This issue of range is an important one, especially if you have come to this exam
at all ill-prepared. If you know one text in great detail, then it might be better to
focus on a question that allows you to showcase this knowledge. In this case
question (b) might appear a better bet than (a).

So what is question (a) about? With luck you will be thinking that this is clearly a
narrative question. So a factor in deciding if this is the question for you is how much
you know about narrative theory. It is specifically the techniques of storytelling that
you will need to use to answer this question. So a good starting point might be to
make a list of those that you can remember. The sort of list you might come up with
is as follows:

- character and character typology

- conflict

- point of view

- enigmas

- outcomes or denouement

- genre-led

Note that the question is about similarities. This might spark in you the idea that
texts that share common characteristics often belong to a genre. One possibility

offered by this question, therefore, is to consider how genre formulae can determine the use of narrative techniques. Soaps would be a self-evident example.

The choice of texts you might make for this question is also important. You are asked to illustrate your answer with texts drawn from film and/or broadcast fiction. What you are not told is how many texts to use for this purpose. It is, however, best to avoid showing off your encyclopaedic knowledge of film and broadcast fiction, not least because you have only 40 minutes to respond to the question and that is bound to limit how many you can include and still produce a meaningful answer.

What else is there to note about this question? Think about the phrasing 'by those who make film and broadcast fiction'. The question is about the producers of texts rather than about the audiences who receive them. This is an important emphasis because it is encouraging you to look at the construction of films and television fiction, i.e. to consider how these texts have been put together, rather than how these texts can be said to affect their audience. Consider also the phrase 'support your argument'. Your argument is in fact the process of accounting for the similarities. Notice how this implies that the texts you are utilising need to be chosen in order to help explain similarities in narrative technique.

If you decide that this is the essay for you, your next job is to make a plan. Probably the best way to do this is to have a list of narrative techniques you want to consider and a list of texts that you think might be used to illustrate the similarities in these. So on a blank sheet of paper copy out the list of narrative techniques down one side and the put a list of texts you might use along the other. You can then start writing ideas and drawing lines to match up some of the techniques and ideas with the texts you have chosen.

Don't forget the focus of this question is: narrative techniques – similarities – texts. Make sure that this is your focus throughout your answer. Show you know the theory by illustrating it with texts.

So maybe question (b) is going to be a better bet. The first thing you should notice is that this looks on the surface a more complicated question than the previous one – complicated in the sense that it requires a couple of readings before it is clear what is being asked.

As we have said in the introduction to this section – don't be easily put off by questions where the demands are not immediately obvious to you. If you take a little time wrestling with this question, then its meaning should become obvious. So be prepared to take a little time and trouble teasing out what you think the question is getting at before you decide whether to have a go at it or not.

Here is the question again:

(b) 'Film and television fiction texts are always based on contemporary issues and attitudes.'

How far do you agree with this statement? Support your argument with a detailed reading of one film OR one broadcast fiction text that you know well.

What it is asking you to do is to consider how far it can be said that one film or broadcast fiction text you have studied is based on contemporary issues and attitudes. Clearly you need to know what is meant by 'contemporary issues and attitudes'. A contemporary issue can be taken as any matter of concern that is prevalent in today's society. So at the time of writing this might be any issue from terrorism through to the quality of school dinners. 'Attitudes' is clearly even broader but you will realise that we are in the realms of ideology here. Attitudes are prevailing ideas within our society, for example the different ways in which the country might feel about the health service, the war in Iraq or even the number of reality TV programmes broadcast.

So the question is asking you to explore how a moving image text is based on such ideas. A soap opera might be seen as a barometer by which social concerns and attitudes can be measured. The storylines of soaps are frequently seen as a reflection of those issues which our society is concerned with, for example teenage pregnancy or gender issues. Some texts that you may have studied will be less obviously concerned with such contemporary concerns. A historical romance or costume drama might seek to explore the concerns of another period in history for example. Although this may the case on the surface, it is often possible to dig deeper into a text and find that it is rooted firmly in contemporary issues despite seemingly depicting a different time period. Science fiction films set in the future can often be seen to reflect our contemporary concerns or neuroses even.

How you tackle this question needs a good bit of thinking through. If you have just one text that you have prepared and you feel you have to fit it into the framework of this question, then don't forget that this is a 'how far do you agree?' question. It does leave the door open to the answer: well not at all really. Note too the key phrase 'a detailed reading'. You are being asked for a close examination of the text. This close examination needs to take place in light of the statement about contemporary issues and attitudes. You are free to agree or disagree. The important thing is that you show you have a good knowledge of the texts and can relate the ideas in the text to the issue in the question.

This is a timely point to remind you that you should not spend a lot of time in this question describing the text you are considering. So many students fall into the trap of delivering detailed and ultimately boring plot summaries, thinking that this is detailed reading. If you don't know what a reading is by now then go back and read Part 2.

Of course if you have prepared properly for this exam, you will have more than one text under your belt ready to apply to this question. If you have, then choosing the right one is crucial to producing a good essay here. Probably the most appropriate response is to find a text that does to some degree exemplify the significance of contemporary issues and attitudes and then use a detailed analysis to show how this is the case. Such an approach is ultimately bound to prove much easier than trying to rehearse the reverse argument. Of course, if you are very clever and clued-up, the argument that says, although a text is set in another time period, it says a lot about contemporary society is going to be a good one provided you can sustain it on the basis of your knowledge of the text.

DOCUMENTARY

THE TOPIC TITLE AND ITS IMPLICATIONS

The title 'Documentary' is simple enough. The challenge perhaps is to recognise what is encompassed by the term, all that it might mean, and, from that, what is really relevant here.

What exactly is documentary? Is it a genre? Or a style? When can a programme be fairly called a documentary? What are its defining characteristics?

Find five television programmes that you would classify as documentaries from current listings magazines.

Brainstorm up to five features that define docs.

Try to write these up as a one-sentence definition.

ACTIVITY

It is possible to dispute even the form that documentaries take, but for the purposes of MED2 you are expected to consider its audio-visual forms – most likely television, possibly film and least likely, though entirely relevantly, radio.

Sometimes, in working towards a definition it can help to think what documentary *isn't* rather than what it is! One defining aspect is its relation to fiction or truth. Docs are factual in that they are concerned with 'real life' events or issues. But one problem students often experience is that as soon as they begin to define documentary they (or their classmates) find examples that seem to disprove the definition. For example, it seems safe to say that docs don't contain fictional characters played by actors. But of course some historical documentaries do bring past events to life in a way very similar to this. Many docs use actors for reconstructions. Drama docs clearly do use actors.

Nevertheless it is important not to get so bogged down that you can't see generic distinctions clearly: *EastEnders* is *not* a documentary, *Panorama* is. So far so good!

It's worthwhile to work out, in terms of forms and conventions, how we know that this is true (see grid opposite).

The points you make in the grid should give you a good indication as to some key forms and conventions of documentaries. *Panorama* has been a key flagship documentary strand for the BBC for decades and it has changed little in terms of form and style. This should confirm that as a television genre documentary is a clearly developed genre with highly predictable forms and conventions. We will explore this issue further later in the chapter (p. 98).

More complex is the way that the documentary form has evolved to affect other genres and maybe even to create new ones. In this respect the development of documentaries can be seen as closely tied to notions of 'the real'. For example, one defining convention of documentary programmes and films is the use of 'actuality' footage – filmed events that would have taken place even if the cameras weren't there. Typical of this sort of material is camcorder footage of disasters or crimes shot by witnesses. Such footage is often recognisable by its poor production values and amateurish appearance – the footage may be grainy, shaky or poorly lit. Shot distances may be ineffective, sound may be distorted and there may be no or little evidence of editing. Such material often finds its way into news items and it has come, conventionally, to signify realism, though of course it is still very much a mediated version of reality. Some of the technical aspects of actuality footage have also become a stock-in-trade convention of dramas such as *Casualty* or *London's Burning*, where the producer is trying to convey a crisis situation 'authentically'. In this sense documentary can be thought of as a *style* that can be used by and can affect a variety of genres.

Realism is always a problematic concept in Media Studies because no more can ever be offered than a representation of the real, whilst at the same time the text is often trying to convince the audience that it is a 'slice of life', of unmediated reality. This tension is nowhere more apparent than in the case of documentary and

Forms & conventions	*EastEnders*	*Panorama*
Camera work		
Narrative		
Sound		
Subject matter		
Target audience		
Scheduling		

will be discussed in greater detail in the course of this chapter. However, we can say that documentary at least charts, or documents, real events.

Here originates the notion of *cinéma vérité* or fly-on-the-wall techniques. These techniques are long established in both film and television but have more recently gained a new lease of life in the form of so-called reality TV shows featuring 'ordinary' people undertaking 'everyday' tasks. The speech marks should indicate a degree of scepticism about this.

So how close is the connection between reality TV and documentary? Well, certainly there's a place for discussing such shows within this topic area but their relationship to documentary as a form, style or genre is a complex one that needs careful handling.

Big Brother, though clearly a far cry from *Panorama* generically, does share a number of its conventions, e.g. fly-on-the-wall filming, voiceover narration (in the Channel 4 edited versions of the show). The use of a studio psychologist in some editions arguably bears some comparison to the use of experts in documentaries and lends the show some gravitas.

Some critics have argued that the documentary form has been rejuvenated by the phenomenon of reality TV which is currently to be seen everywhere in the schedules. Indeed you may want to argue this for yourself, though you must show an awareness of the distinctions between these shows and other, more traditional documentary forms.

In cinema too documentary has more recently experienced a renaissance, with political exposés achieving mainstream distribution deals and independent productions such as *Super Size Me* destabilising corporate giants and developing extended distribution patterns through word of mouth and popular demand! Highly personal and biographical memoirs have also received high-profile backing, e.g. *Tarnation*, made by John Caouette for $218, shot over a 20-year period. The film's official website tells how the project developed from amateurish beginnings to winning high-profile industry awards (http://www.wellspring.com/movies/text.html?page=press_book&movie_id=56&PHPSESSID=06c45d48e8ef1faa2f3f437a36ee5351).

It appears then that 'documentary' can mean many things and has changed significantly over time. Your answer in this topic area must reflect your awareness of this.

SPECIFICATION DEMANDS: WHAT DO I NEED TO COVER?

For this topic area six specific demands are outlined. These are likely to affect the way the topic is taught and how you approach your revision and exam preparation. Here they are in brief:

- Analysis and evaluation of a range of documentaries using the key concepts.

- Forms and styles of documentary (e.g. docu-soaps; fly-on-the-wall; personal; investigative; drama-documentary etc.). Appropriateness of style to content and intentions.

- Analysis and evaluation of documentary techniques (e.g. selection and compression; relation of sound to image; editing; use of narrative; function of narrator; set-ups; effect of camera and crew; entertainment functions etc.). Debates around these issues.

- Positive values of documentary (e.g. educative; informative; illuminative; empathetic, social and political functions of documentary etc.).

- Historical contextualisation of documentary practice through the study of two documentaries made before 1990.

- Institutional issues and debates around contemporary television documentary. Evaluation of current trends and tendencies.

When reading the specification demands, the first thing that is highlighted is the notion of the range and variety of the genre, as mentioned above. Some terms should, by now, be becoming old friends, e.g. 'analysis', 'evaluation', 'key concepts'! As discussed in the Advertising and Marketing chapter (p. 141 below), your analysis of documentaries is likely to focus on media language, representation and values and ideologies and you will evaluate these in the light of target audience and institutional context.

In preparation for the exam you must ensure that you are equipped with *a range* of documentaries that you have analysed in some detail. You need to determine in advance how this range might be achieved. Aim for variety in:

- *Institution*   UK/US, public service/commercial
- *Audience*   mass/niche, populist/highbrow
- *Content*   political, social/cultural
- *Style*   expository, fly-on-the-wall

You might make a grid of the documentaries you have viewed to ensure that it is a wide-ranging selection. Use a current listings magazine to identify a range of documentaries and make off-air recordings of a selection if possible. Don't forget film, and even radio too, to provide a range of forms. Complete dossiers for each programme you watch but keep these fairly brief and to the point for easier revision.

Here is a selection of templates you can use to keep manageable notes on the documentaries you watch. They can also be used to revise how much you can recall about these texts. Notice how much explicit reference there is to the key concepts in the templates. Try to keep these in the forefront of your mind as you are watching and making notes – they will be useful to you in terms of picking up marks in the exam. See pages 99–101.

The second specific topic demand refers to the 'forms and styles of documentary' and lists several of these. We have already alluded to the fact that there is some debate about the status of documentary as either a genre with a set shape and structure and predictable conventions or a style or 'look', a series of techniques or effects which can be applied in many (generic) contexts. In order to address this specific demand you need to show your awareness that documentary techniques can be combined and structured in different ways to produce programmes of very different sorts. Compare, for example, the docu-soap *Ladette to Lady* with the investigative documentary strand *Dispatches* and, in turn, with the drama docu-mentary *Ahead of the Class* starring Julie Walters as a headteacher saving a London school from closure. You may not be familiar with these three examples, but you should be able to identify key differentiating characteristics between these sub-genres or styles. All document factual material but in very different ways: through fly-on-the-wall footage or actuality footage and interviews or using actors and script based on real events.

Before leaving this specific demand let's discuss the final part of it: the requirement for you to show awareness of the *appropriateness* of the style to content and intentions. This is an evaluative task that requires consideration of Audience and Institution. It isn't enough then to describe content – though you should be able to refer to it in some detail – what is more relevant is a discussion of the content to validate, even justify the chosen form and style. For example, popular reality TV shows are sometimes condemned for borrowing some documentary techniques without having the 'weight' or seriousness traditionally associated with the genre. It is at this point that arguments about appropriateness must be brought to bear and you must be on your guard about making value judgements without taking such considerations into account. The makers of *Celebrity Love Island* require its content to be graphic and salacious and its style to be accessible and interactive

Documentary Dossier

Name of Doc:

Broadcast: **When**

Where **Institution**

Duration

Key Conventions
(Choose 4 or 5 noting any significant including absent conventions or atypical ones)

Target Audience

Representations: **Who? Where? How?**

Values/Ideologies

Is It a Documentary?

Conventions   Prog 1   2   3   4

Tick wherever the conventions apply

Actuality footage

Fly-on-wall

Archive footage

Visible recording

Talking head

Interview

Use of experts

Vox pop

Witness testimony

Reconstruction

Voiceover narration

Graphical info

Make a key to show which programmes relate to the grid. You might extend this activity by writing up examples of each convention in action in each programme.

Have I Watched a Range of Docs?

Note briefly information under each heading to cross-reference the range you have covered.

	Prog 1	**2**	**3**	**4**	**5**
Institution					
Audience					
Content					
Style					
Values					
Representations					

if it is to appeal to its target audience in its chosen scheduling slot and make money via advertising and audience voting. But at what point does this cease to be a valid argument to justify the 'reality' these shows offer us?

Press articles on this issue abound. One example from the *Guardian* is offered below.

"Big Brother damages our health"

David Wilson
Saturday August 13, 2005

Do Kim and Aggie, of How Clean Is Your House?, believe that offering people a washing-up rota and some sound advice about vacuuming will resolve the underlying issues that created the piles of filth, newspaper mountains and unmade beds? Does Gillian McKeith think that berating the obese and showing us the content of their 'bad' diets can overcome the billions spent by the food industry to get us to eat junk?

Are people suffering from obsessive compulsive disorder (therapy has become the new vehicle for reality TV) really suitable subjects for entertainment?

Each programme maker will insist that the welfare of their contestants is uppermost, and that they have a whole bank of psychologists waiting in the wings to offer support and counselling. Well, where were they when Kinga was drunk and tipped over into onanism? Why didn't they intervene to prevent Craig from continuing to grope Anthony when the latter was drunk and when he wanted Craig to stop? Might it be that – despite what it says in the British Psychological Society's code of conduct – the need to satisfy the programme makers outweighs the service they should be offering to their clients?

Big Brother has reinvented itself as soft porn, presenting behaviour we'd condemn as antisocial if we saw it in Faliraki or in the high street on a Saturday night as entertainment. The issue here is to think through where all of this will end. What are the unacceptable limits of reality TV? Would we not draw the line at watching someone being tortured, or even executed. I hope so, but then again when footage of Timothy McVeigh's execution was available online, or when it was possible to log on to sites showing the beheading of hostages, there seemed to be an unending number of people willing to watch.

You need to work out for yourself where you stand on this issue of appropriateness, ready to debate it in an exam question, should the need arise.

So how can you best prepare for this specification demand, given the emphasis on a variety and range of styles? The simplest answer is probably to ensure that you have prepared examples for each of the listed forms and styles but this isn't the best approach because:

- The list isn't exhaustive ('etc.').
- Styles date (docu-soap much less common now).
- You don't really need five prepared examples for the exam.
- The list possibly oversimplifies the different documentary forms and styles.

What's more important, we think, is to take on board the basic principle that documentaries of different sorts clearly exist and to differentiate between them in terms of form and style. Textbooks will give you help with this, but be prepared for the fact that each will take a different approach and this can be confusing. As noted before, the test really is how far you can take this material and fashion it to your own purposes.

NOTE

Try these textbooks:

P. Rayner, P. Wall, S. Kruger, *AS Media Studies: The Essential Introduction*

Roger Martin, *TV for A Level Media Studies*

Joe Nicholas, John Price, *Advanced Studies in Media*

The list in the specific demand refers to three approaches to documentary film-making:

- investigative aka journalistic, expository
- fly-on-the-wall aka observational
- personal.

Some authors identify other approaches and you can, of course, discuss these too. However, as these are mentioned in the specification it's important that you are clear about them, and it's worth dwelling on each in a little more detail. We will take these three approaches in turn.

Investigative

One of the roots of documentary film-making is investigative journalism. Traditionally television documentary strands often developed as a result of the limited scope news programmes provided to deliver investigative stories in any depth. *Panorama* is currently trailed on the Sunday evening news on BBC1, underlining this close relationship.

Such programmes document and offer analytical comment on contemporary political or cultural happenings. Increasingly, the documentation underpinning these shows consists of some undercover operation using secretly recorded footage. Recently there have been exposés of the Royal Mail and the NHS in this vein.

Key conventions here include the use of interviews of witnesses and experts and the use of statistics to prove hypotheses. Voiceover narration is also important in making sense of what is being documented and providing some sort of coherent narrative.

Fly-on-the-wall

Documentaries using this approach display an apparent unwillingness to intervene in what is being observed. They appear to document by holding the camera up to a subject and allowing events to unfold. There has been an explosion of documentary film-making of this sort over recent years, due in large part to institutional factors that will be discussed below (p. 121). Populist reality TV shows such as *Big Brother* broadly fall into this category. A range of mainstream shows observing cultural trends can also be included, e.g. the . . . *From Hell* series or *Who Rules the Roost*, where parents are observed struggling with the everyday challenges of caring for small children.

These shows make use of conventions such as talking heads and, fairly obviously, actuality footage. But beware: many of these shows construct very artificial scenarios for their participants and then film the events that result as though they were naturally occurring. Strictly this isn't actuality footage because the events wouldn't have happened whether the cameras were there or not, indeed they are occurring precisely and solely for our edification or entertainment! Furthermore, continuity editing and a minimal, unobtrusive, narrative track seduce us into believing the authenticity of what we are observing, though in fact it is highly mediated.

Personal

What is documented here is material that is in some way definably personal to the film-maker. Home movies can, in a sense, be considered personal documentaries! By drawing the audience in to connect with and respond to material of the most intimate personal nature the film *Tarnation* can be seen as a remarkable example of this form. What marks these documentaries out from others, more commonly, is the presence of the film-maker as a personality within the programme. This might involve him/her being in shot, even addressing the camera, or being heard on the soundtrack. Most likely their involvement will be a crucial aspect in our appreciation of the subject of the programme, though this may significantly affect the issue of objectivity and bias.

Perhaps the most famous documentary film-maker to work in this style is Nick Broomfield, but this approach has been adopted by others very successfully, albeit in a less off-beat way. In *Super Size Me* (2004) Morgan Spurlock positions himself as a highly personal centrepiece in an exposé of US fast-food consumption and its effects. The film essentially charts his experiments with the effects of living on food solely from McDonald's, and his personal health becomes a metaphor for that of the nation.

Some critics have argued that the documentary genre has experienced a 'dumbing down' over recent years and that this technique of person-alisation is part of that process, where abstract hypotheses and objective investigation are replaced by personalities to whom the audience can more easily relate and respond.

Is there a counter-argument to this view? Can you articulate it?

ACTIVITY

When it comes to viewing actual programmes, however, the distinctions outlined here may not seem so clear-cut. Increasingly it seems the elements of one form blend with another so you might find it helpful to organise the documentaries you have studied and prepared in relation to their form and style. For example, *McIntyre Undercover* is investigative but involves personalised elements; *Wife Swap* is observational (fly-on-the-wall) but includes some investigative features; *Dispatches* is a heavyweight investigative strand but adopts other techniques: e.g., in *Beslan* (21 July 2005) it used extensive archive footage of a terrorist attack on a Russian school in an observational way with minimal commentary and analysis (see p. 112).

This specific demand also refers to two hybrid forms, docu-soaps and drama documentary. In both cases documentary techniques are blended with conventions of other popular genres to make new, marketable formats. This serves to underline the extent to which documentary has shown durability and versatility in adapting to a modern media environment.

You should, as part of your exam preparation, rehearse the ways documentary techniques have been combined with other genres. Try to have examples at hand which illustrate this principle in action. The grid on page 107 should help you to identify how different documentaries cross boundaries between one genre and another.

Most media text books will provide you with definitions of these generic hybrids and some give case study examples, though these quickly date and you are really better off finding your own examples.

Docu-soaps are rather out of vogue currently, having lost out to the reality TV format. However, docu-soap conventions can still be observed in episodic shows such as *Holiday Showdown*, the . . . *From Hell* strand and the magnificent *Wife Swap*.

The third specific demand refers to the analysis and evaluation of documentary techniques. It should be clear by now that these are the building blocks through which other key concepts and assessment objectives can be addressed. You should show understanding of each of the eight 'techniques' or aspects referred to in the specification, and others beyond these.

You might approach this by finding examples of each technique in the documentaries you have watched and studied, but remember that it is the analysis and evaluation of the techniques that is being assessed. This involves asking complex questions of texts. Not just the what, where, when but *how* and *why*, and this takes you back to the important considerations of appropriateness and effectiveness.

You might find it helpful to complete a template when viewing documentaries. This could serve as a reminder of what to comment on. Certain techniques may be notable through their absence or the fact that they don't conform to a 'norm' you previously established.

	SOAP	DOCUMENTARY	DRAMA
CONVENTIONS			
EXAMPLES	Docu-soaps	Drama-docs	

Another point that shouldn't be overlooked about this particular specific demand is the inclusion of reference to the way certain techniques can provoke and inform debates in the topic area. This is the extra demand of MED2 over MED1: a requirement that you use theories to articulate debates relating to specific topic areas. Though less important than the analysis of texts in relation to key concepts, this is an important differentiator of your grasp of the topic and your ability to respond to the specific demands of the exam question.

So what debates exist around documentary techniques?

Looking at the list of techniques it seems that the debates centre on intention and appropriateness and, in particular, how these relate to the notion of 'realism'. Documentary, perhaps more than most genres, seeks to offer us a window on the world, to document truthfully. This is underlined by notions such as fly-on-the-wall or *cinéma vérité*. It is vital that you show the examiner that you are alert to the use of techniques to beguile us into thinking that what is offered is 'true' or 'real' in some absolute sense. Take every opportunity to show your awareness that in documentary, as in every genre, mediation is taking place and that the techniques used are affecting the events they depict.

Work through the grid opposite which lists the techniques from the specification demands. Add any others you can. Check your responses here with the completed version in Appendix 2.

The next specific demand is closely related to the debates about techniques, discussed above. As you will have found from completing the grid or looking at the completed version of it, each documentary technique can be seen to have positives and negatives attached to it: the pro and con of debate. You need to get into the habit of formulating arguments on 'both' sides about all the aspects of your media study – take nothing at face value!

This specific demand is about the 'positive value' of documentary, and some such values are listed on p. 99 to help you.

This is an intriguing part of the topic area. Students, in our experience, make value judgements about texts quite naturally but this demand isn't about saying this documentary was 'good' or that another was 'boring'. It's about recognising that documentaries do have functions and effects beyond 'simple' entertainment. Therefore, ensure that you have plenty of ammunition to address, even debate, this notion of positive values should it crop up in the form of an exam question.

TECHNIQUE	ISSUE	DEBATE
Selection/compression	Not whole truth. Somone selecting what's important and what's not. Who? Preferred readings. Bias	But . . . otherwise docs would be boring, shapeless, undramatic.
Editing		
Use of narrative		
Relation of sound to image		
Function of narrator		
Set-ups		
Effect of camera/crew		
Entertainment		
Functions		

As you work your way through this chapter you should be reviewing your notes on documentaries you've already watched and hopefully adding more examples by watching programmes being screened currently.

You need to consider what 'positive values' different documentaries might have. Try to ensure that you are able to comment on each of the values listed in the specification, with reference to textual examples – though it is likely that one programme will support more than one value.

Consider whether there's a connection between documentary form and style and our perception of these values. Many popular reality TV formats receive scant critical attention and negative press coverage. Teachers too, in our experience, are often damning of such shows. Don't be afraid to debate this issue forcefully in your exam answer. After all, the term 'positive value' is in itself making assumptions about the function and purposes of our media consumption. So what if we are only diverted by or escape into a programme for half an hour? Is it being implied that this isn't a legitimate function of documentary film-making?

Is it a contradiction in terms to escape from reality by watching a reality TV show?! Here are a couple of examples that illustrate our approach to this specific demand.

Dispatches is a Channel 4 documentary strand in the expository or journalistic style. It features current affairs topics which might have developed from news items and is quite 'heavyweight' in focusing on international issues, often less accessible to a mainstream audience.

The target audience is likely to be ABC1 graduates, predominantly male with a reformist stance, a social conscience.

One programme, screened on 21 July 2005, was entitled *Beslan* and focused on a terrorist attack on a Russian school in which 350 people died. The audience's expectation might be that they would learn about the motivation for the attack, its perpetrators and what happened to them, the reaction of the authorities at the time and since. The audience might have expected to be *informed* and *educated*.

In fact the programme focused on the three days of the terrorist siege using archive footage from the event and extensive talking heads of those involved. The narrative was highly emotive – unsurprising perhaps given that it concerned the death of so many children – and the audience were invited to *empathise* with the plight of parents and teachers through moving personal testimonies. Drama was produced as the audience awaited the outcome of the siege and the fate of the loved ones of those speaking on camera. It worked on a powerful emotional level because the *empathetic value* was very strong. Actuality footage of concerned relatives waiting for news outside the school was used to develop a sense of drama and emotion.

So, what of our original expectations and assumptions about this documentary?

The fact that many men were featured in the actuality footage but none spoke to camera in interview mode forced us to revise our assumptions about target audience. The material seemed to have received a more feminised handling, though the reporters or film-makers are both male. For example, next to nothing was learnt about the Chechen rebels who attacked the school or what became of them. The actions of the Russian government were described, and lies they told were demonstrated, but these weren't probed. We were *informed* of the events of the tragedy but not really *educated* about its causes or effects.

Perhaps coincidentally, the show was screened only days after 55 people died in terrorist bombings in London. This documentary reinforced the feelings of threat that attack had produced. After watching it one felt more helpless in the face of the threat of terrorism. It is surprising to find the *empathetic value* so strong in a 'hard news' expository documentary.

Another interesting example is *Super Size Me*, the US feature film documentary about the effects of fast-food culture. What 'positive values' are found here?

The film frequently offers factual information in the form of graphics and cartoon stills, vox pops and interviews with the film-maker's doctors, so we are *informed*.

The fact that the film-maker undergoes a radical change in diet, the effects of which are monitored in the film, is *educative* in that we see the effects of the fast food in a very immediate way. Equally, it is an *illuminating* mechanism – the personalisation is effective in helping us to see a more abstract and gradual global problem in a tangible, graphic and immediate way.

The film did perform a social and political function in that it allegedly was single-handedly responsible for McDonald's offering more healthy options as part of their regular menu, in an attempt to reverse the negative publicity produced by the film. Quite how significant the film will be in changing consumer and corporate attitudes and government policy in the longer term remains to be seen.

The extent to which the film provoked *empathy* is perhaps dependent on the individual's attitude to fast food. The film's tone was rather hectoring – as though the audience was being told what to think. The styling of McDonald's as arch-villain, with reference to Play Places weaning poor children from urban environments into a fast-food addiction, seemed rather extreme to us; as did comparisons with litigation against cigarette manufacturers. Of course, in some ways this is a deliberate attempt to generate drama and strong feelings in the audience, but it could be said to militate against empathy for some.

The artificiality of the 'experiment' conducted in the film is also a strength and a weakness. The voyeur in us wants to see the extreme effects of the experiment but it also lets the audience off the hook, secure in the knowledge that these effects don't really apply to us because we don't eat fast food in this way.

This rather begs the question of who the target audience is for this film. Just before the experiment begins the film-maker's girlfriend is seen to cook a delicious vegetarian meal of fresh ingredients. Is this a reflection of the target audience and if so isn't the film merely preaching to the converted? What about the millions who enjoy an occasional Big Mac, or, worse, allow their children a Happy Meal?

It is beyond question that documentaries have the power to effect change for the better. Several have been instrumental in bringing to light miscarriages of justice or raising the profile of an issue and so affecting the public consciousness or government priorities. Some examples are *Who Bombed Birmingham?*; *An Explosion of Guilt*; *Why Lockerbie?*; *In the Name of the Father*.

The next specific demand of this topic area is unique in the specification in that it requires you to consider historical context by studying documentaries of the past. It is stipulated that two documentaries made before 1990 are studied. If you have done this then you should be equipped for this aspect of the exam. However, in practice this aspect of the topic area causes difficulties for students, teachers and examiners alike. Which two documentaries and why those two?

The phrase 'documentary practice' in the specification implies that documentaries were made in a different way before 1990, but is this true? It seems arguable at best.

Even looking as far back as *Nanook of the North* (1920) one is struck less by how different and more by how similar it is to modern documentary film-making.

More recently, the work of a key documentary auteur such as Nick Broomfield is distinctive less because of the historical moment at which it was produced than because of the maverick quality of the film-maker who has in fact worked in similar ways across decades.

Clearly then this is a potentially vexed area. However, as you will see from looking at past exam questions, at most one question in the pair refers to this specific demand. Even then there tends to be an option to use two contemporary docs if you prefer. For example, January 2004:

(a) Analyse two documentaries, one of which must be contemporary, that you believe to be of particular interest in the development of the documentary genre.

AQA 2004

The final specific demand is important because it relates to the key concept of institutions and returns to the question of issues and debates flagged up elsewhere.

It's worth noting at this stage that all the topic areas refer to institutional considerations and the consequent debates. You may find it useful to compare material from other areas. For example, look at the debates listed in the advertising chapter below (p. 146). Many of these issues may be transferable to your work on documentaries.

Thanks to the current institutional climate, documentary has experienced a real rejuvenation. Digitalisation has had a huge impact from the point of view of both production (small, portable cameras which can adjust sound and light levels digitally) and the commissioning and scheduling of documentaries. Historically, slots of time in the terrestrial schedules were dedicated to factual programming. The networks were obliged to fill these but often did little beyond this. The explosion of capacity caused by digitalisation and a consequent fragmenting of the audience created a voracious appetite for cheap, popular programming by public service and commercial producers alike.

Populist documentary formats have sometimes been described as mere schedule fillers but they have come to fill gaps in ever more creative and ratings-winning ways – witness the prime-time slots achieved by numerous docu-soaps and varied forms of reality TV.

The increased availability of CCTV footage and ability to produce hidden recordings with reasonable production values has also benefited the genre. Channels such as History and Discovery turn out documentaries on a seeming factory production line basis and the much maligned *Big Brother* in 2005 completed a sixth successful series, not to mention spawning a host of paler, yet also successful, imitators.

For some commentators though, concerns about the 'dumbing down' of documentaries to satisfy an increasingly commercial, less public-service-driven, climate will remain.

Again, you need to rehearse your arguments and have your examples at the ready. Is a situation where there are more entertainment-driven documentaries a fair exchange for fewer educational ones? Or is the argument more complex than this? We now have *Panorama* and *Big Brother* and some people watch and enjoy both shows!

KEY CONCEPTS: HOW DO THEY LINK TO THIS TOPIC?

As explained in the introduction to this chapter, the need to show and apply knowledge of the key concepts remains of high importance in MED2. It makes sense to analyse texts in terms of their

- media language
- representation
- values and ideologies

and evaluate their effectiveness in relation to

- audience
- institution.

Let's consider each of the key concepts in turn in relation to this topic.

Media language

In an earlier section we discussed the status of documentary as a genre or style. The specification itself identifies a series of key techniques with which documentary is associated. These clearly relate to media language.

You may have encountered documentaries as part of your MED1 preparation or you may have studied its forms and conventions in preparation for your practical production, MED3.

You are likely to be well versed in debates about the definition of the term 'documentary' and exactly what it means in practice. Names such as Grierson, Drew Associates, Flaherty and Nichols may well be familiar to you as writers and practitioners in this field. If not, you might want to research their contribution to theory and practice in this area.

Use the templates provided (p. 102) as a checklist of conventions if in doubt. Make sure you have textual examples at the ready for each key convention. Here are some issues to consider prior to the exam:

▦ Name six conventions that define documentary as a genre.

▦ What can be said about documentaries in terms of their handling of narrative?

▦ How have generic hybrids developed around documentary with specific reference to media language?

▦ If documentary is less a genre than a style, what are the defining techniques of this style in terms of:

❏ camera work
❏ sound
❏ editing.

▦ How does documentary attempt to convince us of its realism or truth through media language?

Don't forget:

▦ Use technical terminology.

▦ Have specific detailed examples prepared.

▦ Styles can be defined in many different ways: be clear about your terminology.

Representation

There are two main considerations in relation to this key concept:

▦ realism
▦ objectivity.

It often seems that these concepts are assumed to apply to documentary, both by producers and by audiences. As media students you know that the presence of any mediating technology militates against realism.

Running several cameras from different angles in a confined space and streaming them live 24/7 is not strictly 'realistic', not the same as being inside the Big Brother house. Note the differences.

However, the technique of using remote and hidden cameras and replaying the footage seems to have come to equate with realism in the minds of many viewers. In shows such as *Police, Camera, Action* or *Crimewatch* CCTV footage is routinely used to solve crimes, enhancing its status as 'real' and 'true'.

Yet the way we are positioned as voyeur, the all-seeing eye, ultimately undermines the realism of the footage. In *Big Brother* we can't experience the house subjectively, as the contestants do. We can see simultaneous footage from kitchen and bedroom, we hear whispered conversations, not intended for others' ears. The supposed omnipresence is important because of the viewer's status as 'judge' and evictor. Nevertheless, we shouldn't be fooled: it only extends so far. The live feed is edited, with the director vision mixing which camera is viewed at any one time, though with the internet and digital television we can make some choices about this. The daily round-up show on Channel 4 which headlines the series and achieves the highest ratings is an edited compilation of the events of the previous day. Obviously this lends itself to the notion of preferred readings and bias, produced by elisions and by the producers privileging one event, character or narrative over another. So much for objectivity!

So documentaries in general – not just *Big Brother* – represent themselves as using 'realistic' techniques, as being 'objective' in their portrayal of reality, but we need to be on our guard about this. As Media Studies students you need to see through the façade of what's being offered and to view in a different way from that which the producer may have intended.

One area where documentary does seem more realistic than its fictional dramatic counterparts is with respect to the representation of people and places. After all, documentaries are set in real locations and peopled

> *by real individuals, not invented characters played by actors with a script.*
>
> *But is the distinction so straightforward?*
>
> *List ways in which the representation of people or places in documentaries might depart from the real.*

The documentary sets out with a 'hypothesis' and a view of its subject. Investigative documentaries may feel duty-bound to represent 'both sides' of the argument in an attempt to appear impartial. However, other documentary film-makers may be less circumspect with respect to balance. In Michael Moore's *Bowling for Columbine* the representation of people and places is clearly biased, though the fact that this is directed against the film-maker's own home country and state may seem to exact a measure of objectivity! Bush and Heston are never offered as anything other than two-dimensional villains, even buffoons. Moore's home state of Michigan is seen to be populated by gun-toting weirdos! The US itself is represented as seriously dysfunctional: Moore's connection of the local armaments factory with the school killings represents a country with a deeply ingrained predilection for violence.

But what of opportunities for self-representation in documentaries? In shows such as *Big Brother* it would appear that contestants can control the way they appear to us. According to Endemol, the show's producers, the contestants are merely filmed according to their actions, implying a high degree of control on the part of the contestant. Yet time and again contestants have complained about their representation.

There is good reason to believe that even at the moment of selection as an entrant to the house their representation is, to a degree, fixed by the show. Indeed, the entrant has been chosen because of some characteristic that they will demonstrably represent. On the day the show begins, short biographies of the contestants are released to the press. Already they are being referred to as some sort of 'type'. For example, Anthony, ultimately the winner of the show, was defined by his job: a 1970s' dancer. This signified 'camp' but also 'cool'!

Values and ideologies

The link between representation and values and ideology is strong, as noted elsewhere (p. 56), for the way the producer represents the world reveals their attitudes and values, the 'preferred reading'. This is strongly evident in documentaries, and may be easier for you to write about here than in relation to other topic areas. Partisan documentaries that make no secret of their 'bias' are particularly useful here. Not surprisingly, where personalisation is strong, e.g. Nick Broomfield or Michael Moore, their values and ideologies are clearly seen.

In terms of your own writing you need to:

- Be clear about the values offered.
- Be clear how these are articulated through media language and representation.
- Consider the significance of audience and institution in relation to this.

But the values and ideologies within a documentary may not always be so transparent. In particular be watchful for the illusion of neutrality or objectivity where, in fact, certain biased attitudes and values are being communicated in 'disguise'. Programmes using fly-on-the-wall techniques are particularly troublesome or interesting in this respect. Shows such as *Wife Swap* or *Who Rules the Roost?* appear objective and even-handed in their representations but closer scrutiny usually reveals a bias towards the values of one party over another, and these are very often middle-class and aspirational. The case of Lizzie Bardsley on *Wife Swap* was an interesting one. Having been 'set up' as a lazy and undeserving scrounger by the programme, followed up and elaborated upon in the *Daily Mail*, she developed a cult anti-hero status and has since enjoyed some success as a television presenter and minor celebrity! Her re-invented persona serves only to point up the bias within her original representation and the hidden nature of that bias. Be on your guard!

If you lack confidence and feel unsure in interpreting values and ideologies within documentaries then think carefully about audience and institutions. What are the dominant values of the group you consider to be the target audience? What is the ethos of the commissioning and broadcasting institution? Presumably they will be reflected to some extent in the documentary.

Audience

This section should be prefaced 'proceed with caution'! Documentaries are, of course, created for specific audiences but in most cases these are unlikely to be as clearly targeted or defined as those of advertising campaigns, for example.

Beware of identifying an audience profile if this is really guesswork. However, there are a few points to bear in mind in deciphering audiences for documentaries:

- What sort of documentary is it? Investigative? Reality TV?

- Scheduling should help. Investigative documentaries such as *Panorama* or *Dispatches* tend not to command peak slots, suggesting niche audiences, though perhaps relatively influential and powerful ones, e.g. professionals, graduates.

- Psychographically, documentaries may appeal to carers (empathetic) or reformers (social and political function).

- Demographically they appeal to more mature males with their emphasis on evidence and investigation, though reality TV shows and docu-soaps reverse this skew.

Certain clues are available to help you deduce target audience but proceed with caution, weighing factors against one another and taking a commonsense approach:

- *Viewing channel.* Each has an identity and slightly different audience profile, though we may of course watch them all from time to time.

- *Schedule slot.* The day of the week, the time of day, the duration of the show, other shows positioned around the documentary all offer valuable insights.

- *Content.* Documentaries in a given strand change their content markedly from one week to the next. This is a generic convention of a documentary series. As a result, these shows are trailed more than programmes in other genres. The content is less predictable and so needs more signposting to a potential audience.

Institution

Institution is often a poor relation among the key concepts but it is a fascinating area in relation to documentary. Traditionally documentaries have occupied an unusual position in the television schedule. Terrestrial networks are obliged to screen documentaries as part of their obligation to meet the needs of a wide range of audiences, though often they have been pushed into minority viewing slots and largely ignored. Conversely, documentaries have sometimes been seen as flagships of the public service tradition, fostering citizenship and informing and educating the audience about important matters of the day that might otherwise have been supressed or overlooked. Costly drama documentaries such as *Who Bombed Birmingham?* played a part in establishing the possibility of a miscarriage of justice in the public mind and, ultimately, in the release of wrongly convicted prisoners.

The more recent history of television documentary has been even more intriguing. With the advent of satellite, cable and finally digital technology the industry saw a massive increase in capacity (i.e. the space needing to be filled by programmes) while the television audience remained static. Consequently television audiences have gradually fragmented and ratings for individual shows have declined. The race was on to find appealing formats that could be produced cheaply!

This 'race' affected new and old producers alike. Sky and Discovery, for example, needed to lure audiences away from the habit of the terrestrial network, whereas the BBC and ITV saw their once-captive audiences drifting away and commercial imperatives increasingly outweighing public service ideals.

Documentary presented a solution to this problem because, particularly in the digital age, it constituted cheap television. Small crews, filming members of the public in everyday locations, rather than using paid actors in studios or exotic locations meant that production costs plummeted. So evolved a profusion of formats with a greater or lesser documentary element. Ironically, it was public service channels with the money up front to dare to be different and possibly fail (BBC) or with a remit to be different (Channel 4) that scored the greatest early populist documentary successes, *Driving School*, *Cruise*, *Big Brother* and *Wife Swap* all having a significant impact. Perhaps the acid test though is to look at how documentary is faring in a truly commercial environment. The Sky network hosts a raft of documentary channels with wall-to-wall programmes on a massive range of subjects. Though still attracting small audiences these programmes often have an international appeal, important in the context of a global corporation and lend the network some gravitas. Sky One is increasingly offering documentaries as a marketable part of its viewing menu, both as stand-alone shows (e.g. Julie Burchill's *Chav*) and as mini-strands or series where collaboration with other parts of the Sky network is clearly evident, e.g. sport documentaries such as those on Jose Mourinho. The commercial terrestrial channel ITV abandoned its long-time investigative documentary strand *World in Action* in favour of the more lightweight *Tonight with Trevor McDonald*. The latter show receives a peak slot and high ratings and is an excellent example of the versatility of the documentary format and its ability to appeal to a wide range of audiences. Anchored by the elder statesman of news presenting Trevor McDonald, it uses traditional documentary conventions such as voiceover narration, archive footage, interviews, expert and witness testimony and statistical evidence. The subject matter though is often rather lightweight and populist with a strong appeal to a female audience. Hammocked between soap operas and *Celebrity Fit Club*, the choice of the effects of the Atkins Diet for one show seemed apt!

It is often claimed that commercial channels such as ITV are less inventive, experimental and risk-taking than their public service counterparts because of the need to deliver ratings reliably to advertisers. The case of documentary seems to constitute an interesting exception. ITV's rather tabloid-oriented C1–D audience thrives on game show and celebrity-driven formats. So in order to jump on the documentary bandwagon ITV needed to find a way to integrate its bankable genres with the documentary form. Shows such as *Pop Idol* and *I'm a Celebrity Get Me Out of Here* are the result. Whilst these shows are far from being documentaries in the traditional sense, they do include conventions such as fly-on-the wall filming, talking heads and interviews. It is notable that shows such as these include an increased element of interactivity via elimination formats with opportunities for audiences to vote for or against contestants. These conventions perhaps provide a narrative hook by which to attract and maintain audiences, all important for commercial producers who use ratings to increase advertising revenues.

So, different institutions will employ documentary forms in different ways, subject to their audience, ethos and aims. It is testimony to documentary's versatility that it routinely crosses generic, stylistic and institutional boundaries.

CHOOSING APPROPRIATE TEXTS

With the exception of pre-1990 texts for historical contextualisation, accessing appropriate texts should not be a problem for this topic area. As discussed above, documentaries are to be found everywhere on television.

If you are lacking textual examples, one week's viewing and recording should suffice. Plan recordings that enable you to cover the range and scope necessary to meet the demands of likely exam questions. You need:

- two pre-1990 documentaries
- one illustrating each key style or form, e.g. investigative, observational, interactive

- perhaps a mix of television and film documentaries

- documentaries broadcast by different kinds of institutions, e.g. public service, commercial

- documentaries for different audiences, e.g. mainstream and populist, niche and intellectual

- documentaries with different functions and purposes, e.g. empathetic, reforming

- documentaries with varied content – this will give you greater range when discussing key concepts such as representation or values.

This starts to look like a very long list! However, if you made a grid you would quickly see that one documentary can fulfil many criteria. You probably don't need more than six shows prepared in depth and maybe a similar number that you might refer to in passing in more general terms.

The pre-1990 examples are more likely to originate from classroom study because they are more difficult to get hold of. That said, textbook research will give you some good leads that you can chase up on the internet.

For feature film documentaries and archive programmes, internet-based DVD lending libraries can be a very useful resource, with their huge back catalogues.

Bear in mind that if you are treating documentary as a style rather than a genre other non-documentary examples can be brought into play. Be careful about how you do this – you need to be absolutely clear about emphasising the documentary techniques. You can see how this might be done in the example we have worked from *Mean Creek*.

DOCUMENTARY TECHNIQUES WITHIN TEXTS OF OTHER GENRES

These days documentary form and style crop up in all sorts of unexpected places within the media and, at their best, can lend greater authenticity and creatively enhance a range of fictional texts.

In Jacob Este's film *Mean Creek* (2005) a group of teenagers take a boat down river in order to get revenge on the school bully, George, played by Josh Peck.

In the opening scene we see George rig up a video camera to record himself playing basketball. When another boy inadvertently disturbs the camera George viciously assaults him. Some of this is seen through the perspective of the video camera and throughout the early part of the film George's 'documentary' version of events operates in parallel with a more traditional omniscient perspective.

Far from being a two-dimensional villain, at home George is presented as a complex character, part victim, part creative introspective. In voice over for his camera footage he explains that in order to be understood he needs to 'document the zillion things going on in my head'.

The documentaries he produces become a tool in uncovering his isolation and, for the audience at least, understanding his character. Later, the footage on the camera proves how he died, not to the audience who were already aware, but to the police and his mother.

Its status as an agent of objective truth is, by turn, reinforced then questioned. For example, when George is in control of the camera in the company of others he is confident, humorous and inventive. He speaks of 'making it on MTV'. In a supreme postmodern irony he believes he can uncover who he is only via the camera, show who he really is to others only through his documentary films.

The film explores the contradictions and ambiguities of our quest to express our individuality yet to be popular with others and to 'belong'. The inclusion of documentary film footage and depiction of George as an amateur film-maker demonstrates the fine line between objective truth and subjective perception which the modern media tread.

A remarkable and unusual example of how documentary techniques can be used to enrich a fictional text on many levels.

Make sure that you present your examples professionally, noting the title of the programme and its writer or director, and the date and channel on which it was broadcast.

Ask the following questions of any text you are considering using – the more of these criteria that the text meets, the better a choice it is!

- Is it contemporary? Aired within the last five years? Or pre-1990, possibly ground-breaking in its time?

- Can you discuss the text within the context of the documentary genre or form with some sense of overview?

- Are you sufficiently familiar with the text to discuss media language and representation *in detail*? Do you have ready access to a hard copy of the text?

- Does this text contribute something different from the other examples you have collected so that you are able to make new and different points with it?

- Have you been able to collect background information that will enrich the exemplification – e.g. background to its production, ratings, information about the subject of the documentary, press coverage about it, etc.

Bear in mind that different sorts of examples will serve you well in different circumstances.

Look at past exam questions and plan out answers identifying appropriate examples. The question of 'appropriateness' will be resolved when you are clear about how you intend to use the text. One documentary might be perfect to exemplify a specific aspect of the topic, so use it accordingly, as we have done throughout this section.

KEY CONCEPTS, ISSUES AND TEXTS

The extra challenge of MED2 over MED1 is the need to integrate theories, issues and debates into the discussion. Planning an answer then should ensure all three elements are included.

Issues ⟶ **TEXTS** ⟶ **Key Concepts**

Remember, you are showing an understanding of texts above all else, so your worked examples must be central to your answer. Next most important, in terms of assessment objectives, and therefore the reward you receive for your answer, is applying the key concepts to the texts. Finally, of least importance, but still necessary, is the integration of theories and debates into your analysis. Of course, in practice all three elements will be melded together, possibly in a way that makes differentiating between them quite difficult.

Let's look at how this might work out in practice:

Explain how documentaries can only give their viewers a mediated view of 'real life'.

AQA January 2004

In this question the theoretical focus is provided: 'mediated', 'real life'. This will require you to engage with the notion of realism and how this is constructed technically in documentaries.

'Viewers' are referred to, so the key concept of audience must be addressed. The 'how' focus gives media language primacy, though representation and values and ideologies can also be fully integrated.

Examples aren't explicitly referred to but their use is implicit in 'Explain how documentaries'. You might well use different examples to illustrate some of the different ways in which documentaries mediate reality.

Let's try another question for comparison:

Describe and analyse **two** documentaries, explaining how each one has been constructed to have particular impact on its audience.

AQA June 2005

This question presents different challenges. This time the textual focus is prescribed: 'two documentaries'. A contrast between them is implied through the reference to the key concept of audience. Comparison of the two isn't a stated requirement, though it might enrich high-quality answers.

Similarly, there is no explicit reference to issues or theories but ambitious, more able candidates will work out how to integrate these. Reference to 'how . . . constructed' is a reminder to focus on the forms, conventions and techniques, i.e. media language. 'Describe and analyse' signals a need for detail in the exemplification but try to meld the two together: Description of the documentaries without analysis won't attract many marks.

So can we predict the style of questions that are likely to come up? Let's have a look at another example:

> Why do people watch documentaries? Support your answer by referring to examples from a range of documentary formats that you feel illustrate the appeal of documentaries to audiences.
>
> AQA January 2005

This seems to be a very open question, which often initially attracts candidates, but beware, these questions have their own challenges. Again, audience is referred to, a reminder of its importance as a key concept. Textual support is defined and related to media language – 'range of . . . formats'. 'Why' implies a more abstract engagement akin to theory. In fact the question implicitly adopts the uses and gratifications stance that media texts meet particular audience needs.

It would be rash to say that it is possible to predict questions but at the same time it is possible to see a pattern emerging here:

- Recognise and explore the key concepts, even if the question doesn't tell you to.

- A theoretical focus may be specified, e.g. realism, mediation, bias. Even where this is the case you still need to develop a debate and integrate relevant theories.

- Audience is a key consideration.

- Textual focus isn't always specified but tends to assume reference to more than one documentary of different kinds. Historical context may be a restricting factor here.

The key is to understand the specific demands of the question. Some elements will be more explicit than others, depending on the question, but you can rely on the fact that every question will require

- detailed textual reference and exemplification

- broad and thorough reference to the range of key concepts

- reference to relevant theories, issues and debates relating to the area of study.

A CLOSER LOOK AT THE QUESTIONS

For each topic area you have a choice of two questions and must answer one of them.

Look at past papers on www.aqa.org.uk and consider the differences between the two questions in each pair:

- Equal difficulty
- Test different aspects of the specification
- Require different sorts of examples
- One example may need to be pre-1990
- Varying focus: broad or more directed.

You need to attempt answers to the different question types to see which suits you better. As a fail-safe, work towards coping with your less preferred style of question! Check you understand the terminology of the questions so that you don't feel uncertain about the appropriateness of your response.

Here are two sets of questions, from June 2003 and June 2005.

EXAM QUESTION

(2a) 'Documentaries can never provide an accurate representation of reality.' With detailed reference to two or more documentaries that you have studied, discuss the validity of this statement.

(2b) 'The biggest stars of contemporary documentary formats are the editors.' (Gareth McLean writing in the *Guardian* after watching 12 hours of unedited *Big Brother* on E4.) With reference to documentaries that you have studied, how far do you agree with this statement?

AQA June 2003

(2a) Describe and analyse two documentaries, explaining how each one has been constructed to have a particular impact on its audience.

(2b) In recent years popular documentary formats have placed people in contrived situations.

> Account for the appeal of this type of documentary to producers and audiences.
> Support your argument with textual examples.
>
> AQA June 2005

Let's consider the different demands of two sets of question pairs.

June 2003:

- Qa: Focus on Representation. Also need to address issues of realism and mediation. Requires debate.
- Qb: the title quote refers to reality TV and *Big Brother* specifically. It also refers to editing (Media Language). The question itself though is broad and opens out the debate to address other areas.

June 2005:

- Qa: straightforward analysis. Two documentaries. Refers to Audience specifically. Comparison possibly implicit.
- Qb: another question referring to contemporary documentary formats. Refers to Audience and Institution.

Note a continual emphasis on recency and detail in textual exemplification. Modern popular documentary is often a question focus so this should be part of your research. Teachers are likely to assume that you watch these shows but you must also analyse them with the same seriousness you would other types of documentary.

Specific key concepts may be mentioned in the question but even where they are not referred to explicitly they *must* be dealt with – the rubric on the front of the exam paper states this.

CHOOSING AND PREPARING TO WRITE

You don't really want to be in a situation where you are forced to answer one question because you are unprepared on the topic material for the other.

See above for advice about preparing examples but ensure you are covered in terms of breadth and depth:

■ A range of theoretical terms and issues should be understood.

■ Some detailed knowledge will be needed.

■ Be prepared to apply that knowledge and 'think with it' so that you use what you know to engage the examiner, construct an argument, generate some sort of debate.

As previously suggested, you should watch a range of documentaries and take notes about them. The question remains, however, how such notes might be built into an exam response. Below is an attempt to take you through that process.

In summer 2005 the BBC ran a short series of documentaries on football-related topics, presumably for those fans feeling at a bit of a loose end during the closed season! Alan Hansen, the former Liverpool player and *Match of the Day* pundit, fronted one of the shows on *Life After Football*. The programme made an interesting case study, particularly from the point of view of representation and values. The programme inquired into what happened to professional footballers when they could no longer play the game to make a living.

Any film-maker, in making representations, necessarily selects and therefore also leaves things out. The organisation of the selected material is also relevant to the film-maker's purposes. This applies as much to documentary films as to fiction films.

The 'drama' or 'hook' of this show resulted from the fact that footballing heroes, previously represented in the media with glamour, success and sporting prowess, were now paraded before the camera in a spectacle of failure: broken marriage, unemployment, etc. In truth their previous representation had been rather two-dimensional; this documentary seemed intent on continuing this trend but in reverse! One former Man Utd and England star was filmed in a truckers' café and spoke with some chagrin of his difficulty in securing a job even as a van driver. Would the audience be horrified by his 'fall from grace' or gratified to find he was 'just like them after all'?

The documentary seemed to hypothesise that the footballer who fails to plan for the future is courting disaster. The show's most complete representation of this 'truth' or, more properly, ideology was, of course, Gazza. Paul Gascoigne, a gifted if rather unstable former England midfielder, spoke of an almost phobic aversion to facing a future not playing football. He was represented by the show as a victim, humbly deferring to Hansen's patronising tone in interview. There was little to see of the practical joker that played such a key part in Gazza's media representation in years gone by.

Set against Gazza in terms of narrative and values was his binary opposite Gary Lineker. Former England centre forward, famously never booked, Lineker represents stability and geniality in his role as *Match of the Day* anchorman. In the documentary we learn that Lineker planned a media career many years before he retired from playing professional football. Indeed, he was apparently nicknamed 'Junior Des', a reference to Des Lynam, a former presenter of *Grandstand* and *Match of the Day*. Gary's forward planning was offered as rather heroic in interview, the questions phrased in such a way as to leave us in no doubt of Hansen's approval of him.

The smug cosiness of that interview between fellow BBC employees on the same show was strongly contrasted with Hansen's conversation with Rio Ferdinand. Walking through woodland with Hansen, his lack of awareness of the topic under discussion was both bemusing and refreshing. Hansen repeatedly tried to turn the conversation to Rio's future plans and encourage him to face up to a future without playing football. Unable or unwilling to contemplate such a scenario, Ferdinand finally turned to Hansen and exclaimed: 'Man, what we talking about this for? It's so depressing!' This exposed the oversimplification of the previous representations and allowed the true complexity of the issue to break through.

So how can this rather ordinary documentary be useful in relation to the examination questions?

EXAM QUESTION

'Documentaries can never provide an accurate representation of reality.' With detailed reference to two or more documentaries that you have studied discuss the validity of this statement.

AQA June 2003

OR

'All documentary makers have a view of their subject matter that they want to communicate to audiences.' By referring in detail to at least two documentaries discuss the techniques documentary makers use to make their views clear.

AQA January 2005

Either of these questions would work with the chosen example, picking up on the issues of representation and values discussed above.

Unfortunately however you can't determine what questions will be set. Looking at the 2005 exams, how useful would our *Life After Football* example be?

Here is a brainstorm and plan answer for the second of these questions from the January 2005 exam.

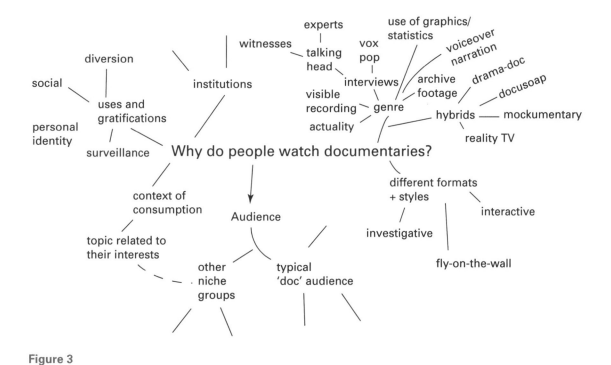

Figure 3

See if you can complete or add to the plan by considering:

- how institutions could be worked in
- the make-up of the typical documentary audience
- which textual examples fit where
- which audiences seek which gratifications.

This is how the plan was developed.

1 The question was broken down into its key components:

■ why   ■ people   ■ documentaries.

2 What you need to include to respond to each question element:

'Why' . . . this can be worked out in relation to the different key concepts. Institutionally documentaries are everywhere in the schedules and hard to avoid! In terms of audience 'why' implies a uses and gratifications approach where audiences make motivated choices about their viewing on the basis of the needs they want to be fulfilled through the media. 'Why' can also be answered in terms of media language and representation via the pleasures afforded by the forms and conventions of the text.

'People' . . . needs to be dealt with in terms of audience. We would need to show that different sorts of documentary attract different kinds of audiences. These audiences could be defined in terms of demographics, psychographics or their interests and priorities.

'Documentaries' . . . Though not explicit, this part of the question needs to be unpacked to show awareness that documentaries are of very different generic kinds and employ varied techniques and styles.

3 Relate these question demands to the chosen examples:

The question refers to 'examples from a range of documentary formats'. A range requires at least three examples. Many more than this and the exemplification may lack detail. If we want to use *Life After Football* we need other examples that will contrast with it. An observational or interactive example such as *Who Rules the Roost* or *Wife Swap* would be useful. A personalised documentary with a strong message, perhaps a feature film, would make a good comparison, e.g. *Super Size Me* or *Bowling for Columbine*.

4 Consider ways in which you can integrate key concepts and issues, theories and debates:

■ Uses and gratifications immediately seemed relevant.

■ Institutional considerations can be referred to in explaining the current popularity of the genre.

■ Realism, though not explicit in the question, should be referred to as a likely appeal.

5 Finally put your points into some sort of order so that a structured line of argument can develop.

■ *Introduction.* Different audiences find different sorts of documentaries appealing because they use the media to fulfil different needs.

■ *Main points.* Traditionally docs provided the gratification of surveillance, informing audiences, generally mature males. *Life After Football* example.

■ Many documentaries, in dealing with political, social and cultural issues, allow their audience to re-evaluate their own identity and values. *Super Size Me* or *Bowling for Columbine* would work here. So would *Wife Swap.*

■ More recently popular reality TV shows combine game-show and documentary elements, offering audiences diversion and an interactive experience. *Ladette to Lady* or *Celebrity Love Island* could be used here, among others!

■ Underline the differences between these shows in terms of their forms and conventions, the techniques they use.

■ *Conclusion.* Cynically, audiences watch docs because they are ubiquitous! However they are also versatile and gratify audiences in different ways. They provide institutions with cheap programming yet are nevertheless ratings winners. Although they are every bit as mediated as fiction texts, audiences are made to feel close to the real with documentaries and this has enduring appeal.

In June 2005 only one of the questions would have allowed us to use the *Life After Football* example:

EXAM QUESTION

Describe and analyse two documentaries, explaining how each one has been constructed to have a particular impact on its audience.

AQA 2005

Here the challenge would be choosing a second documentary with a different audience and a different impact, possibly two different styles or formats. Hopefully, as we reach the end of the chapter you can see that many of the documentaries discussed above would meet that need.

The question doesn't stipulate comparison, so you could write on each documentary separately. The answer would be enriched by some element of comparison, however. Perhaps you could deal with one text and then analyse the second in the light of the first.

A closer look shows that this question is in fact very similar to the previous one: both are looking for you to explain the appeal or impact of different kinds of documentaries by referring to textual examples, and this should be the key consideration in your revision of this topic area.

ADVERTISING AND MARKETING

THE TOPIC TITLE AND ITS IMPLICATIONS

The first point to note about this topic area is the title: Advertising *and marketing*. Some exam candidates treat the topic as being purely about advertisements, with scant attention being paid to marketing, sometimes even when this is an explicit concern of the question!

At least one question in the pair can reasonably be expected to focus on marketing as distinct from advertising itself, though this will not necessarily be the case.

Marketing can, in one sense, be considered to be at the edge of Media Studies as its purposes and outcomes may not produce discernible media products. So in the minds of some candidates the topic may be thought to belong more properly in Business Studies, for example. However, most marketing campaigns will include media texts of some sort.

Furthermore, as audiences become ever more sophisticated media users and perhaps inured to the effects of traditional advertising, so marketeers are becoming increasingly creative – some might say insidious – in their attempts to pitch to us 'through the line' or using 'guerilla tactics', to use industry parlance. The chief executive of one guerilla marketing organisation has this to say:

> Consumers know the difference between traditionally placed media and guerilla-placed media. They know that the type of placement lends to the personality of the brand and that cooler companies or brands go against the grain and do something maybe not so legitimate and that lends to the credibility of certain brands. The message stands out. Media that's guerilla-placed stands out ten times more than traditional media.
>
> Adam Salacuse, CEO of Boston-based Alt Terrain

In this sense marketing can be seen as of prime concern to the contemporary student of the media. *The Essential Introduction* (see p. 257) has a case study on this topic area which should form a sound starting point to your revision.

SPECIFICATION DEMANDS: WHAT DO I NEED TO COVER?

The specification details five areas of coverage for this topic and these are, in themselves, quite revealing. Here they are in brief:

- Analysis and evaluation of a current advertising or marketing campaign using the key concepts.

- Marketing theory, principles and practice.

- Analysis and evaluation of promotional and covert advertising techniques (e.g. sponsorship, product placement, public relations, plugs, etc.). Functions and purposes of different techniques.

- Politics and marketing (role of spin doctors; images of parties and party leaders; political news management; debates around image and substance, etc.).

- The impact of promotion, advertising and advertising funding upon media content. Financial, ethical, professional, public service or audience debates around this issue.

The first, and arguably most important, is the requirement to analyse a current campaign. The importance of approaching this task seriously cannot be overstated. To quote from the Principal Examiner's Report of summer 2004:

> **some candidates lacked the skill of selecting material relevant for the question and wrote pre-prepared, rather mechanistic responses which were not angled appropriately towards the question.**

Instead, what is wanted is:

> **detailed case studies of brands and campaigns**
>
> **close, first-hand study of advertising texts.**

The emphasis here is upon candidates taking the initiative and researching, investigating and reflecting upon the effectiveness of campaigns for themselves, rather than using classroom-based, taught examples.

The most important words relating to this area of coverage are 'current' and 'campaign'.

The title of the unit and the underpinning of it both stress the importance of developing an ability to analyse *contemporary* texts. Advertising is a particularly transient, ephemeral media form – 'old' campaigns, though often the subject of discussion in textbooks, are difficult to experience first-hand and can in any case seem rather irrelevant. Arguably no media form dates more quickly than advertising. As John Hegarty, chief executive of advertising agency Bartle, Bogle and Hegarty, recently wrote in an article for the *Guardian*, 'It's often said in advertising that you are only as good as your last idea. In reality, you are only as good as your next one.'

Writing about current, topical campaigns will not only meet the assessment criteria and impress the examiner, it will ensure that your writing is spontaneous and individual to you and will therefore enable you to display critical autonomy – an important descriptor at the top end of the mark scheme. More on how to achieve this below.

The other important word in the first specification demand for this topic is 'campaign'. Adverts are not created individually, within a vacuum; they are part of a marketing strategy, a campaign, comprising a variety of elements, often crossing media channels. Despite this fact, many students write about individual print and television adverts without any sense of a wider campaign. One reason for this is perhaps that adverts are consumed as individual texts and, depending on the range and amount of exposure to the media at a given moment, a candidate may be aware of only one advert for a given product.

In a lazy mood you might feel you need do no more than 'watch a few adverts' to prepare for this section of the exam. How wrong you would be!

Historically it was quite difficult to uncover industry information about complete campaigns but thanks to the internet this is no longer the case. All advertising agencies have websites, many of which are used as a tool to promote their work. Websites of some very well-known agencies have pages giving information about their client list and showcasing selected campaigns. This not only allows you the opportunity to see or hear the adverts as a complete campaign, but gives information about the background to the campaign, the market situation for the product prior to and after the campaign and the strategy utilised. Some agencies are even aware of their usefulness as an educational resource and devote web pages to students' questions. Clearly this sort of information can revolutionise your work on this unit and make it very exciting to research, though of course it is best to experience adverts in situ, as their creators intended, if possible.

The febrile nature of advertising makes it difficult to be sure of the shelf-life of any recommendations but, with this proviso, some suggestions are offered below:

- http://www.4rfv.co.uk/fulllisting.asp?scategory=4.
  This is a portal with links to websites for all the advertising agencies in the UK. Extremely useful.

- http://www.bbh.co.uk

- http://www.ogilvy.com

- http://www.tbwa.co.uk.

These are some great ad agency sites that showcase their work.

So keep it fresh and up-to-the minute and think big – in terms of a campaign rather than a single advert. These are key differentiators of the quality of exam answers in this topic area.

Another issue to be alert to in relation to this first specification demand is the advertising/marketing distinction. As a rule students find it easier to write about advertising than marketing, perhaps because they have more first-hand knowledge of advertising. However, most advertising campaigns are part of a wider marketing strategy.

Reliable information about up to date marketing campaigns can be difficult to come by for students and teachers. One useful resource is *Campaign* magazine, the trade journal for the advertising and marketing industry. Some libraries carry this valuable resource. There is also an on-line version of the publication called *BrandRepublic* with an excellent archive, but the site is subscription-based and expensive, with limited access for the casual surfer. Even so it is well worth a look as it carries up-to-the-minute news about advertising and marketing campaigns and showcases current ground-breaking or controversial work. News articles it runs, though available to the non-subscriber only in brief, can provide you with sufficient information to research further for yourself via other websites and the site runs a bulletin where articles can be viewed in full for free – but only for a short time. Store the site as one of your 'favourites' and scan it regularly:

- http://www.brandrepublic.com/news

Another line of enquiry with regard to marketing campaigns is to explore those agencies which specialise in so-called 'guerilla' tactics. These agencies utilise non-traditional methods of advertising, rejecting conventional media channels and seeking to affect the audience without them necessarily being aware that they've been the target of an advertising pitch. Two excellent websites for this purpose are:

- http://www.cunningwork.com
- http://www.altterrain.com.

Not only do they showcase work with key clients, they include rationales about the principles behind their work and its effectiveness.

As you were perhaps already aware, a campaign is made up of several elements and is very often cross-media in its range and scope. Your exam responses and in particular the textual examples therein should explicitly reflect your awareness of this – discuss 'the campaign' rather than 'the advert' in isolation.

Remember the importance of the key concepts in your analysis and evaluation of textual examples from within your topic area.

Deconstruct the campaign in terms of

- media language – sub-genre, narrative
- representations
- values and ideology.

Evaluate its effectiveness in terms of its

- target audience
- institution – client, positioning within the media.

Marketing theory, principles and practice is the second area of coverage for this topic. This highlights the importance of marketing within the topic. Many media textbooks include information about marketing theory.

Prime among these is the so-called *marketing mix* or 'Four Ps': product, price, promotion, place. In addition you may be conversant with theories such as the Lifecycle of a Product (sometimes known as the Boston Matrix) which tracks the different phases of a product's 'life' and the different marketing strategies needed at each stage. Or the AIDA model which considers the different appeals advertising needs to make to us in order to achieve a sale. Still other writers theorise about advertising from the point of view of psychology (John Berger) or in terms of techniques of persuasion (Graeme Burton).

Get to know your theories well and practise how you intend to use them, applying real, current examples to the theories in some detail. Wholesale regurgitation of theory is not what is required, rather the application and evaluation of the ideas in relation to well-chosen examples.

Further emphasis is placed on methods of advertising in the third specified area of coverage – promotional and covert techniques. Four methods are identified:

- sponsorship
- product placement
- public relations
- plugs.

These very different forms have in common the fact that products or services or individuals are promoted by means other than that of buying air time or space in a conventional way.

Sponsorship and plugs in talk shows for example are fairly easy to spot as a form of promotion, but public relations and product placement are perhaps less easy to identify in action – indeed this is an express part of their intention, that they are advertising in disguise, hence 'covert'.

Q: When is an advert not an advert?

A: When it's public relations!

As mentioned above, as the audience increases in sophistication and so perhaps becomes desensitised to traditional advertising, so advertising agencies are turning to more unconventional, 'hidden' methods to make an impact. Event-based marketing is growing in popularity – the cunningwork.com site features campaigns for Mini and Tango Apple using this technique. This involves live events in places where maximum publicity and word-of-mouth business can be achieved, for example city-centre squares or night-life districts of major towns. Attempts to make advertising seem personalised are ever-more ingenious, with the use of post-it notes, answer-machine messages and viral on-line marketing.

Even where advertising is more traditional, marketeers seem to be looking for a distinctive edge.

The latest campaign for Yorkie chocolate, featuring the slogan 'it's not for girls', has been running for some time. Conventional print and television advertising attracted free publicity in the form of a feminist backlash debated in the broadsheet press. Most chocolate is of course marketed towards children or women, and Yorkie is one of a number of brands which have chosen to artificially limit their target audience and present this exclusivity as a unique selling point.

The story becomes more interesting when one considers that the product sponsors the Sky Sports flagship Saturday morning soccer show *Soccer AM*. This show, with a cult following among football supporters especially from lower leagues, features a sketch-type advert either side of each ad break – significant given that this is a three-hour live show. Each sketch points up the soccer savvy of men at the expense of their clueless female counterparts – though this is blatantly biased for comic effect. This sexism or laddism is mirrored in the content of the show which features a soccerette who parades a catwalk in little more than a t-shirt for the gratification of a group of male supporters in the studio.

In fact the relationship between product and show bears closer scrutiny. Contrary to the apparent sexism of some parts of the show is the anchor Helen Chamberlain, a knowledgable and no-nonsense Torquay supporter who plays a key role in all aspects of the show's success. How does she relate to the 'it's not for girls' tag-line? One could argue that the slogan is in any case tongue-in-cheek and that what it really seeks to do is market itself distinctively in a saturated sector. Women who reject conventional notions of 'girly' femininity might well relate to the more ladette representation that Helen offers. Indeed, her role is arguably one which gains the respect of male and female football supporters to a greater extent than that of Gaby Logan, a female anchor for ITV's football coverage, for example. Yorkie's sponsorship of *Soccer AM* can be seen as more complex in this light and as possibly extending the target audience in ways that might not have originally been envisaged.

Yorkie provides a good example because it is interesting from a number of viewpoints:

- The original marketing strategy is distinctive and unusual.
- Conventional advertising accrued free publicity (intentional?).
- Sponsorship enriches our understanding of the strategy and includes an adaptation of traditional advertising to grab attention.

So there is a mixture of conventional and covert methods interlinking here to good effect.

The final two areas of coverage detailed in the specification both relate to issues and debates within the advertising and marketing sphere, one focusing on politics, the other on the effect of advertising on the media's output itself.

Clearly it is important that you can rehearse these debates in your answer in detail and with some confidence but the detail and topicality of your exemplification of these debates will remain a key differentiator in the quality of your answers.

Election campaigns are now painstakingly stage-managed, employing leading advertising agencies, and the public relations management of political parties is a permanent year-round activity. With increasingly low turnouts by voters, ironically perhaps partly caused by the parties' perceived manipulation of the media, ever more extreme tactics are being used to provoke a reaction. Prior to the May 2005 general election the problem facing the Labour government was the fear that their voters would not bother to vote, believing victory was assured. To tackle this problem advertising agency TBWA and campaign adviser Alistair Campbell decided to run a print advertising campaign featuring two Jewish Conservative ministers as flying pigs. Immediately the Labour Party was accused of anti-semitism and many column inches and much air time on television news was devoted to discussing the campaign. Clearly in the eyes of the campaigners the drawbacks of being accused of racism were outweighed by the promise of mobilising voters with the added bonus of much free publicity. An example of all publicity being good publicity?

The establishment of digital technology in both the print and audio-visual media industries has enabled an expansion of capacity and consequent fragmentation of the audience and market share that has handed greater power to advertising, with increasing proportions of costs being met (and profits delivered) from advertising revenue. Thus the power of advertising to influence media content has arguably never been greater. Consider for yourself the ways in which this could be said to be true. We will return to this issue later in the chapter.

The specification identifies five areas of debate that a consideration of this issue might produce:

- financial
- ethical
- professional

- public service

- audience.

Though ultimately all those areas of debate can be linked together you should be able to make discrete, distinct points about each effect and to discuss these points in terms of 'pro' and 'con'.

One common pitfall is that students present advertising as an ogre that governs and affects media output in negative ways without acknowledging its positive effects.

Use the grid on page 144 and fill it in as far as you can. The gaps could form a focus for your revision.

See Appendix 3 for the completed version of this grid.

Once you feel fairly secure on the nature of the debate in relation to each point, you need to ensure that you have appropriate textual examples to illustrate each. These are less likely to be campaigns as such and more likely to be examples garnered from press articles or from your personal consumption of other media output and impact of advertising upon it that you've observed. You might find it useful to keep a log or diary about this.

Get into the habit of checking the *Guardian* newspaper's Media section each week, either in printed form or on-line. Even scanning headlines should alert you to any notable debates or controversies. Magazines such as *Heat* and *Now* can be a valuable resource in terms of the ways in which celebrities attempt (not always successfully) to control their public image and manage news about themselves. The management of PR events such as the Rebecca Loos/David Beckham affair or the changing public perception of Abi Titmuss might form an interesting focus of discussion. The use of reality TV programmes to re-launch fading celebrities or as a vehicle for presenting them positively as an antidote to more negative press coverage could also be studied.

Finally in relation to the coverage required for this topic area is the issue of regulation. Although this is not explicitly referred to, it is implicit in the reference to 'professional' considerations within the debate about advertising's effect on media content. The advertising industry is largely self-regulating, with various codes governing different media. The regulatory bodies exist to check that agreed guidelines are not breached. The strength of the system is that most advertising abides by the code guidelines, so regulation is minimal and light. Problems arise when advertising is passed for consumption but then causes offence among the

ADVERTISING: EFFECTS ON MEDIA CONTENT		
Area of debate	**Pro**	**Con**
Financial		
Ethical		
Professional		
Public service		
Audience		

audience. If complaints are received, advertising may be withdrawn but many commentators argue that the publicity the advertisers attract in the interim is temptation enough for many to seek to breach the code guidelines. The notion of notoriety can have a positive PR value for many products – another example of all publicity seeming to be good! When complaints are received in sufficient numbers the ASA or broadcast equivalent will review the complaint and adjudicate upon it. These adjudications are posted on the website and form another useful place to find out about topical, controversial advertising.

Pot Noodle has been a repeat offender in this respect over recent years and forms an interesting case study. The product has been associated with fairly inventive advertising since its launch in 1979. However in 2004 the brand image went in a new direction with the 'slag of all snacks' campaign. Adverts depicting Pot Noodle being surreptitiously consumed in a red light district were quickly condemned and eventually withdrawn but not until a cult word-of-mouth following had built up for the ads themselves which could be viewed on the Unilever website.

More recently the seedy, sexy image of Pot Noodle has been further developed with the 'Have you got the Pot Noodle Horn?' campaign involving a man with a bulge in his trousers relieved after eating the product. By 18 March 65 complaints had been received, triggering an investigation by the ASA. The advertising agency HCCL/Red Cell has defended the campaigns by arguing that they appeal to the core market of 16–24-year-olds and are broadcast after the watershed. It is clear that, with this target audience at least, using risqué humour is a positive advantage as a marketing technique, even (or especially) if that means courting controversy. The product has long been thought of as an unhealthy fast food that might be considered 'shameful' by some. The creative directors have used these negative product features and turned them into a benefit using the well-worn strategy of humour and sex in combination. Not surprisingly given the target audience, the campaigns have had some unexpected spin-offs.

Arguably the advertising has attracted criticism because of the product's broad appeal and targeting towards young people. Advertising around children tends to be a highly contentious matter. Even the advertising of an innocuous product like Robinson's Fruit Shoot by Britvic has received much criticism and complaint.

As part of the 'Get Good' campaign, targeting 7–11-year-olds, Britvic decided to take over ad breaks with three-minute 'features' encouraging kids to 'get good' at a variety of activities including making music, gymnastics and skateboarding. The adverts imitate the forms and conventions of the sub-genre of children's television programmes showing them how to acquire various skills or learn about unfamiliar sports. At first glance the programme doesn't appear to be an advert, though the product is alluded to in various ways through the course of the feature. The product logo appears several times and one child drinks from a Fruit Shoot bottle. Brand Controller Jonathan Gatward says, 'Get Good from Robinson's Fruit Shoot is an interactive programme for kids which genuinely helps them to learn how to get better at activities that they enjoy.' The television campaign is teamed with a sophisticated on-line campaign which consumers must visit to claim 'instant' prizes from the bottle packs. The campaign has helped the product achieve unprecedented sales growth of 32 per cent and the product is estimated to be worth £70 million. The success of the campaign has produced a good deal of negative press for the product, however, on grounds that the sophisticated marketing ploys linking high-sugar food to active sports are cleverly designed to engage children's attention. Each 300ml bottle of Fruit Shoot contains more than 170 calories! Arguably there is an ethical issue at stake here . . . What do you think?

KEY CONCEPTS: HOW DO THEY LINK TO THIS TOPIC?

As explained in the introduction to this chapter, the need to show and apply knowledge of the key concepts remains of high importance in MED2.

In relation to the advertising and marketing topic we have already suggested that it makes sense to analyse texts in terms of their

- media language
- representations
- values and ideologies

and evaluate their effectiveness in relation to

- audience
- institution.

Let's consider each of the key concepts in turn in relation to this topic.

Media language

Much of your knowledge from MED1 can be brought to bear here.

You need to deconstruct your chosen examples in relation to the forms and conventions of their medium, genre or sub-genre.

Use technical terms in the same way as you would in analysing a MED1 text. In addition you might want to think about conventions that specifically relate to advertising and tend to cross media boundaries, in particular the distinctive relationship between text and images, e.g. anchorage, slogans, tag-lines, logos.

Draw up lists of the distinctive characteristics of adverts in each medium – film and television, radio, print. You could then consider how far these features cross over from one medium to another. For example, can narrative be said to operate in print advertising? We think it can and have argued as much in the MED1 section in our reading of the *Knight of Passion* advert for the film *King Arthur* on p. 61.

In the diagram on page 148 common features of print adverts and their conventional layout are outlined.

Consider the order in which we pay attention to these items. Do they all necessarily receive our attention? The same amount of attention? Do we return to some items? Do we simply read from top to bottom, left to right, or is the 'narrative' more complex?

Even narrative theories could be applicable, e.g. Lévi-Strauss's binary oppositions or Barthes's action and enigma codes. Many adverts present their product as delivering an idealised equilibrium with the world without the product being depicted, even implicitly, as 'disrupted' or less pleasant. Because of the limitations of a print advert narratorially some adverts offer two adjacent 'realities', one with and one without the product. The audience is positioned to choose the reality featuring the product and representing a Todorovian equilibrium. In Proppian terms the product is often presented as hero in solving the audience's problem. Alternatively the product is a donor or provider that enables the audience to become a Proppian hero. Try to find print adverts where these theories can be seen in action.

It's well worth thinking about how the target audience is shepherded through the advert, remembering the aim in view is usually to persuade us to buy something we didn't know we needed!

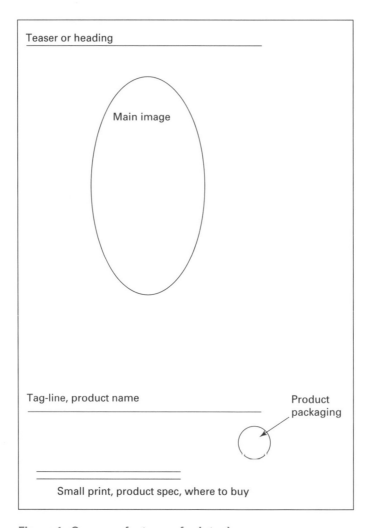

Teaser or heading

Main image

Tag-line, product name

Product packaging

Small print, product spec, where to buy

Figure 4: Common features of print ads

The AIDA model is helpful here and can be considered in narrative terms. The theory states that successful advertising captures our Attention, retains our Interest, generates Desire and calls us to Action. Use the chart opposite to log analysis of adverts in terms of AIDA.

Does the advert take us through these stages sequentially or is there a feeling that more than one of these stages is occurring at the same time?

It might appear easy to pick up marks by showing your knowledge of media language with reference to chosen example adverts. However, beware. Don't fall into the trap

PRODUCT	ATTENTION	INTEREST	DESIRE	ACTION

of simply describing adverts' language features. Analysis is required – recognising technical features and ascribing or assessing their significance. It is the application of your knowledge to ideas, theories and debates that defines this unit and makes it distinctive from MED1 in its demands. As with MED1, ultimately it is the synthesis of your knowledge and understanding in different areas that will characterise a successful answer because then creditworthy points are more densely packed and economically expressed; your response is more complex and sophisticated.

Representation

Representation can be considered a particularly fruitful area of investigation in this topic area. The brevity and consequent compression of meaning of advertising texts means that they are especially vulnerable to the charge of stereotyping, as they attempt to communicate complex messages to a potentially unsympathetic audience clearly and very quickly.

Adverts represent people and places in ways that aim to persuade us to buy products and services. Idealised versions of reality are often offered to beguile us into believing that by buying the product we can access that lifestyle.

In order to attract a target audience adverts often feature members of the target group – indeed this is one way in which students often identify target audiences in advertising and other media forms. However, this relationship between target audience and representations within the advert is often more complex than at first appears. As a general rule adverts in the UK are peopled by white, slim, conventionally attractive individuals, free of blemishes, disabilities or unique distinguishing features. If you doubt this, keep a tally chart across several ad breaks of what representations are seen. These representations might be considered as a 'window to the future self' of the target audience, to use John Berger's phrase. The audience aspires to this representation and the product is positioned to aid them in achieving that goal. The prejudice inherent in such depictions of the 'ideal' has been the subject of much criticism of advertising, though the industry tends to counter with the argument that they merely reflect the ideologies of the surrounding culture. This forms an interesting and important point of debate for you.

There has been some, rather limited, evidence of a backlash against these 'idealised' representations. Campaigns have been run by both Marks & Spencer and Dove where the 'real', 'flawed' beauty of women is accentuated and associated with the brand. Presumably the logic here is that women will feel reassured by the representations they see, and their relief from the pressure to aspire to an unrealistic representation is expressed in a more positive attitude to the brand. Interestingly, M&S quite quickly abandoned their strategy but Dove have developed theirs into a full-blown 'Campaign for Real Beauty'.

In the examples above the positive associations of the product are positioned as a reward for the audience. Occasionally the reverse is true and a failure to use a product is depicted as a punishment to be avoided at all costs. The horror of being discovered to have BO or the impossibility of cleaning the stains from clothes or the home are all examples that spring readily to mind. Financial products are also often marketed around the idea that you would be foolish not to take advantage of a particular deal. The Norwich Union insurance company has recently run the campaign 'Are you ready for tomorrow?' where a young person is seen to age, using CGI technology, as they talk down the importance of good financial planning.

As you can see in this example, values and ideologies are also being represented. Here the notion that the young are carefree and thoughtless of the future is encoded and perhaps implicitly even approved of. The target audience is not perhaps this 'careless youth' but a slightly older group who have begun to age and not yet taken steps to protect their future through pensions etc. This attitude is implicitly criticised through the threat of the tag-line 'Are you ready for tomorrow?'

Values and ideologies

It can be seen then that, in respect of advertising and marketing in particular, the link between representation and values and ideology is strong. Though one of the more complex key concepts, it has a central importance here.

Marketeers seek to persuade us to buy by convincing the target audience of their 'need' for the product. If you are familiar with Maslow's Hierarchy of Needs you will be aware that many products and services which are advertised do not relate to the primary needs of food, shelter and warmth. They relate to higher-order needs such as esteem and self-actualisation. The strategies used in many campaigns are designed to lock into and exploit the target audience's attitudes and values, their aspirations or insecurities. Indeed, their perception of self or self as they would wish to be ('future self') can be of vital importance in the sales pitch of modern advertising campaigns.

Some items are sold by playing on the audience's fears and suggesting that the product can meet key primary needs, for example it has become fashionable to sell family cars on the basis of their safety features.

Modern manufacturing industry relies on persuading the audience to replace and upgrade products regularly. Its advertising therefore aims to convince us of the obsolescence of older-style products. There is a continual emphasis on 'new' and 'improved', and ideologically this can be seen as a prop to consumerism and capitalism.

The link between marketing and capitalism is, after all, a deep-seated one. Marketing is above all about creating an appetite to purchase goods and services, even where there is no apparent need for them.

To write about values and ideology for this topic area, think in three ways:

- the attitudes and values of the target audience (see below: audience, psychographics)
- the values of the institution: its ethos, image
- wider cultural attitudes and values. Show awareness of dominant, alternative and oppositional ideological positions on a variety of issues.

It is extremely important to institutions that they maintain an image which reflects positively upon them. When David Beckham was accused of extra-marital affairs in the media none of his many sponsors complained. Nike on the other hand demanded a public refutation of claims that Wayne Rooney had thumped his girlfriend Colleen. Reebok adverts alluding to rap artist 50 Cent's gangster background via his nine gunshot wounds have been withdrawn in the UK after complaints, though they have been deemed a success in the US. (See discussion of this later, p 165.)

These examples tell us about a complex pattern of cultural values affecting advertising and marketing institutions. Host institutions too are concerned to protect their reputation and image – some magazines refuse to carry controversial advertising. The ASA tries to predict likely public reaction to campaigns on the basis of their perception of the target audience's attitudes and values, thereby protecting the host from any unnecessary adverse publicity. Unfortunately it could be argued that it is in the interests of some products to court controversy because of the additional publicity that their notoriety is likely to attract.

Audience

It has probably already become clear that audience is a very important key concept for this topic area. The campaigns you explore and exemplify must be evaluated in relation to the target audience for whom they were designed.

The notion of a campaign designed to appeal to 'everyone' is a contradiction in terms, though candidates often fail to recognise this, perhaps out of laziness or because they lack the confidence to properly delineate the audience targeted. At the very least you should be aware that our needs, priorities and preferences change according to age, gender and class or wealth, for example. The marketing industry is underpinned by an awareness of this and has a myriad means by which to segment the population into meaningful audience groups.

The audience can be defined by a series of variables. These include

- geographic
- demographic and
- psychographic variables.

Psychographics refers to the definition of the audience according to attitudes they display, and has grown in popularity. This is perhaps as a result of society becoming more mobile and more fluid in terms of status. Psychographics enables marketeers to pitch to niche groups on the basis of their values and ideologies, regardless of their gender or where they live. Psychographic groupings tend to be known by acronyms, e.g. *Whanny*, *Dinky*. The term *Yuppy* originated here. Some are nicknames that quickly reveal the attitudes and values held, e.g. reformers, grey panthers. Some are rather cruel, e.g. lombard (Loads Of Money But A Real Dickhead)!

The golden rule is that for any campaign you discuss you should make sure that you identify the profile of the target audience and evaluate the campaign's effectiveness with this audience in mind. Be aware of primary and secondary audiences, especially where a child audience is involved.

So how can you find out the target audience for a particular campaign?

- Begin with finding out about the product or service – its cost, its features and its benefits.

- Note where the campaign appears – which magazines or newspapers? Around which television programmes? Does it feature on radio? Which station? What time of day? If it's in the cinema, before which films?

- You could conduct your own primary research about who is aware of the campaign and who has responded to it.

■ If the campaign is controversial, or ground-breaking, it may have received press coverage – this may indicate the target audience or re-route you to other websites that will tell you.

■ If you can find out which agency created the campaign this may help you.

■ It may have attracted complaints and so feature on the ASA website or on BrandRepublic.

One problem that advertising creative directors face is that their advertising is intended for a specific target group but is consumed by many outside that group. Offence may be caused to those who are not part of the target audience. Some campaigns that are controversial escape withdrawal on this basis. In your evaluation of a campaign you should show awareness of the likely response of (a) the target group and (b) those outside that group who may respond positively to it.

The effectiveness of advertising is judged not solely on improved sales but also in terms of awareness raising. Terms such as 'penetration', 'reach' and 'recognition' refer to the effectiveness of advertising in these terms. Indeed, some market leaders, such as Tesco or McDonald's, advertise partly to keep the brand at the forefront of the audience's consciousness and to maintain a positive perception of the brand.

The points above serve to underline the central importance of the notion of audience to the marketing industry, and so to your answers on this topic.

Make sure you know the difference between mass and niche audiences, and can differentiate between target audience and audience appeal, and between the broad appeal of the product as compared to the group targeted by a specific campaign.

Institution

The relationship between text and institution is quite complex in respect of advertising and marketing. Usually institution equals producer but in advertising the notion of 'producer' is blurred by the processes of mediation that take place from product through to publicity. See the diagram (Figure 5) relating to a washing powder advert on the facing page.

See also the marketing strategy diagram (Figure 6). In the marketing strategy example, the institutional context is complex and multi-faceted: many media institutions are involved in providing publicity but the 'producer' of the strategy is the publicist, for example, Max Clifford.

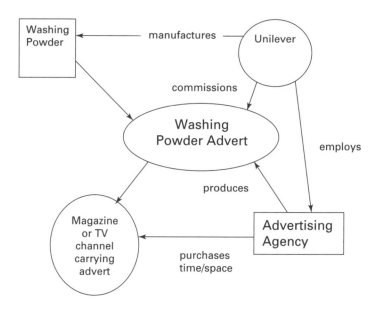

Figure 5: Who 'produces' a print ad?

Figure 6: Who 'produces' a marketing strategy?

In a few rare cases one might consider the celebrities themselves to be the architect of their own public relations and to take on the character of an 'institution' in their own right. The Beckhams form an interesting case study in this respect.

In the case of 'kiss 'n' tell' stories or exposés of celebrity lifestyles by former employees, publicists will factor into the equation rebuttals by the celebrity or even possible court action. In such cases the publicist is concerned not merely with the content of the story but with the reaction it receives, which may generate much more publicity. Recently a judge refused the Beckhams an injunction against their former nanny's revelations, on grounds that they themselves had previously courted publicity. This decision in turn provoked many column inches in terms of what this might mean for the future press coverage of other celebrity lifestyles.

Again, the institutional situation can be seen to be a very complex one that can produce a great deal of relevant and interesting discussion.

CHOOSING APPROPRIATE TEXTS

The importance of having appropriate textual examples has been stated and re-stated in this chapter.

Ask the following questions of any text you are considering using (the more of these criteria that the text meets, the better a choice it is!):

- Is it contemporary? Aired within the last five years? Modern, possibly ground-breaking?

- Can you discuss the text as part of a campaign with some sense of overview?

- Are you sufficiently familiar with the text to discuss media language and representation *in detail*? Do you have ready access to a hard copy of the text?

- Does this text contribute something different from the other examples you have collected so that you are able to make new and different points with it?

- Have you been able to collect background information about the campaign that will enrich the exemplification – e.g. statistical data, complaints, sales, press coverage about controversy, etc.?

Bear in mind that different sorts of examples will serve you well in different circumstances. Look at past examination questions and plan out answers identifying appropriate examples. If you can't manage this yet, consider what *sorts* of examples might work well:

- Which medium?
- Which genre?
- Which products or services?
- Which target audience?

To turn the argument on its head, you may feel that you have done lots of research into certain campaigns and so you are *determined* to use them, come what may! In this case you would need to look at the past exam questions and work out how you can weave these campaigns into your essay or argument.

As a fail-safe, ensure that you have a minimum of two marketing campaigns prepared, as distinct from those using traditional advertising.

Four prepared advertising campaigns seems a minimum, covering different target audiences, different media (at least print and television, and if possible radio and Web). Try to include some guerilla tactics. Try to include campaigns for both products *and* services or issues. For the latter charities or health campaigns can be useful.

Consider including examples of other media-based advertising, e.g. of Sky or BBC digital services. The advantage of this is that it gives you yet another way to discuss institutions! The information you research may well be useful elsewhere in the qualification, certainly more so than finding out lots about soap powder!

Present your examples professionally – collect dates of the campaigns being launched, information about the commissioning institution (manufacturer) and advertising agency. As you research, log information such as this coherently. Keep a note of useful URLs. Any really useful material you find, print off and store with your notes and highlight key statistics and quotes from it.

There's a plethora of information out there. Merely logging on to Guardian Unlimited and checking 'Advertising' and 'Marketing and PR' in the Media section will enable you to accrue a massive amount of useful information. So, be single-minded. You can't research everything so choose and then stick to your guns. Though if something really exciting comes along you might make an exception . . . !

Keep an eye on the media in the broadest sense whilst preparing for the exam – check the news daily and if you have Sky News check showbiz and celeb news in particular. Read *Heat* or *Now* or *Closer* and scan the papers each day, especially media sections in the *Guardian* or the *Independent*. Watch snippets of talk shows such as *Richard and Judy*, *Jonathan Ross* or *GMTV* – they should give you a good clue about who's plugging what. In your wider viewing note who's sponsoring which programme and what you see as the significance of that deal. Target audience? Values of the programme? Perceptions of the product?

If you watch a US film or television programme, note any instances of product placement. Manufacturers pay to have their products placed prominently in media texts in the US, though this is not permitted in the UK at present – here brands are chosen at random and undue prominence should not be given to one brand. Where you do notice product placement, ask yourself what is gained from the association of that product with that text. Be on the look out for anything controversial or ground-breaking.

Try to find out what campaigns are making an impact with different audience segments . . . Ask your parents or grandparents or siblings which adverts, running currently, are most memorable for them.

Think about who is having a PR nightmare currently or who is getting very positive press. In the week of writing this, Michael Jackson (court case), Wayne Rooney (did he thump Colleen?) and Jessie Wallace are all in difficulties. José Mourinho (still the Special One) is on the up. Look at current political coverage, whether there is an election or not. What kind of PR are the party leaders receiving? Or the parties themselves? What issues are producing good and bad publicity for them?

At the time of writing Labour has just won a third consecutive general election. They received good publicity on the economy but negative publicity on Iraq. The Liberal Democrats capitalised on that as an anti-war party but couldn't convince the electorate of their ability to govern. The Conservatives scored positive publicity on immigration but still were perceived as a 'nasty' and 'old-fashioned' party by many.

KEY CONCEPTS, ISSUES AND TEXTS

The extra challenge of MED2 over MED1 is the need to integrate theories, issues and debates into the discussion. Planning an answer then should ensure all three elements are included.

Issues ⟶ **TEXTS** ⟶ **Key Concepts**

Remember, you are showing an understanding of texts above all else, so your worked examples must be central to your answer. Next most important, in terms of assessment objectives, and therefore the reward you receive for your answer, is applying the key concepts to the texts. Finally, of least importance, but still necessary, is the integration of theories and debates into your analysis. Of course, in practice all three elements will be melded together, possibly in a way that makes differentiating between them quite difficult.

Let's look at how this might work out in practice:

EXAM QUESTION

How important is the role of direct advertising in 'the marketing mix'?

Illustrate your answer by referring to one recent campaign that used a variety of strategies, including direct advertising, to reach its audience.

AQA June 2003

The theoretical aspects are given to you in this question: 'the marketing mix'. The focus for your examples is also specified: 'direct advertising' (meaning paid-for, not covert), 'recent' and 'variety of strategies' (one advert or medium won't really do here).

The key concepts are not explicitly referred to, except for 'audience', and it is down to you to give them their full weight in your plan and your answer.

Let's try another question for comparison:

EXAM QUESTION

Describe, giving detailed examples, some of the potential advantages for advertisers and marketers of **one or more** of the following media outlets:

- Television
- Radio
- Print media
- Outdoor advertising
- Cinema
- Internet and new media technologies.

AQA January 2004

This question presents different challenges. This time the textual focus is prescribed – the list of media forms – but there is some scope in terms of what you focus on and in how much detail.

You must focus on 'advantages' but theories and issues and the key concepts remain implicit. This is in fact a more 'open' question than the previous one, though that can be a blessing or a trap.

So can we predict the style of questions that are likely to come up? Let's have a look at another example:

EXAM QUESTION

'Research has shown that many groups, for instance young people, do not respond to traditional advertising strategies when making their consumer choices.'

Discuss in detail some recent promotional strategies that have been developed in response to such challenges.

AQA January 2005

Here a specific audience is specified, though only as an example, perhaps leaving the door open to a discussion using other audience segments.

Traditional strategies are set against other (guerilla?) strategies but the textual focus is vague, specifying only 'recent' and 'some strategies'.

Again, theory and key concepts (except 'audience') are implicit.

It would be rash to say that it is possible to predict questions but at the same time it is possible to see a pattern emerging here:

- Recognise and explore the key concepts, even if the question doesn't tell you to.

- Generally you are asked to discuss one campaign, but the focus of that might be specified in terms of audience or form.

- A theoretical focus may be specified, e.g. branding, marketing mix. Even where this is the case you still need to develop a debate and integrate relevant theories.

The key is to understand the specific demands of the question. Some elements will be more explicit than others, depending on the question, but you can rely on the fact that every question will require

- detailed textual reference and exemplification

- broad and thorough reference to the range of key concepts

- reference to relevant theories, issues and debates relating to the area of study.

A CLOSER LOOK AT THE QUESTIONS

For each topic area you have a choice of two questions and must answer one of them.

Look at past papers on www.aqa.org.uk and consider the differences between the two questions:

- equal difficulty

- test different aspects of the specification

- require different sorts of examples

- one has a marketing focus

- one focuses on traditional advertising, the other on covert or guerilla methods

- varying focus: broad or very directed focus.

You need to attempt answers to the different question types to see which suits you better. As a fail-safe, work towards coping with your less preferred style of question!

Check you understand the terminology of the questions so that you don't feel uncertain about the appropriateness of your response.

Let's consider the different demands to two sets of question pairs:

EXAM QUESTION

(3a) Describe, giving detailed examples, some of the potential advantages for advertisers and marketers of one or more of the following media outlets:

- Television
- Outdoor advertising

■ Radio

■ Cinema

■ Print media

■ Internet and new media technologies

(3b) 'Standing out from the crowd is an essential part of any advertising campaign.' (Meg Carter in *The Guardian* 28/01/02)

Discuss this statement with detailed reference to a recent campaign of your choice.

January 2004

(3a) By referring in detail to a recent campaign that presents a strong brand identity show how brand image is important in advertising and marketing.

(3b) 'Research has shown that many groups, for instance young people, do not respond to traditional advertising strategies when making their consumer choices.'

Discuss in detail some recent promotional strategies that have been developed in response to such challenges.

AQA January 2005

January 2004:

■ Qa: focus on media forms and the advantages (and constraints, implicitly) of different media.

■ Qb: A broad question hung on a quote. Deceptively simple? The required focus here is on reference to a campaign *in detail*. A response here would need careful planning.

January 2005:

■ Qa: refers to a theoretical concept: branding.

■ Qb: refers to a specific audience grouping and highlights the issue of contemporaneity.

Note a continual emphasis on recency and detail in textual exemplification. The key concepts tend not to be mentioned in the question but *must* be dealt with – the rubric on the front of the exam paper states this.

CHOOSING AND PREPARING TO WRITE

You don't really want to be in a situation where you are forced to answer one question because you are unprepared on the topic material for the other.

See above for advice about preparing examples but ensure you are covered in terms of breadth and depth:

- A range of theoretical terms and issues should be understood.

- Some detailed knowledge will be needed.

- Be prepared to apply that knowledge and 'think with it' so that you use what you know to engage the examiner, construct an argument, generate some sort of debate.

Below is an attempt to work through an analysis of an advertising campaign and how it might form the basis of an answer to question (3b) above from January 2005.

Reebok's latest advertising campaign, entitled 'I Am What I Am' features a wide range of popular culture icons making statements about their attitudes and values. One advert which received a lot of additional publicity featured rap artist 50 Cent.

Media language

The advert was designed as a magazine double-page spread. The advert also appeared as a shop window display and as a billboard advert. The left-hand page comprises a close up image of rap star 50 Cent. The shot is fairly dimly lit with a key light front right. It is a shot of his face and upper body. No sportswear is visible. He wears a vest and camouflage print cap with peak to the side. In addition he wears a large diamond chain and stud earrings: 'bling'. The right-hand page comprises a background of a close-up police fingerprint document. This is overlaid with two quotes in different typefaces. One, the upper, is in a very plain font with the 'o's distinctively blocked out. It is ascribed to 50 Cent. The other obtrudes into the left-hand page and is in a larger, ornate, archaic, maybe gothic, font – this is the title of the campaign and is common to all the print adverts. The new style Reebok logo is also prominent. All the text is in white and layered over the images. A very restricted colour palette has been used with tones of black, white, grey and khaki predominating. In the television advert 50 Cent recites numbers from one to nine – alluding to the number of times he has been shot. This reference caused the withdrawal of the television version of the advert in the UK after complaints by the Mothers Against Guns campaign group.

Reebok is a leading sportswear brand, though it lags some way behind other brands such as Nike and Adidas, especially in terms of marketing itself as a leisurewear brand. It is notable that this campaign features no explicit reference to sport either in imagery or text. Similarly the notion of a product as such is absent.

The connotations of the media language used are suggestive of macho street culture. A black anti-role-model is used as an icon. His violent past is alluded to, though it remains unclear the extent to which he is being offered to us as a victim of gun crime or as a glamorised exponent of it.

Audience

The primary audience seems likely to be young males, predominantly white, though emulating black culture. The notion of 'cool' is extremely important in the marketing of sportswear to young people. In the past so-called 'cool hunters' have been employed to discover what is at that moment thought to be cool on the streets and to promote specific brands as cool with these opinion-leading groups. The use of a black rap icon such as 50 Cent appears an attempt to short-cut this cool hunting process. 50 Cent is currently very cool with four singles in the US top 20. If Reebok use him to endorse their products their hope is to become cool by association.

His notoricty and controversial public image make him a threatening figure for the secondary audience of older adults and parents. It is perhaps for this reason that the references to gun culture are relatively opaque. This forms a restricted code of intertextuality that can be read only by insiders, making the adverts more powerful for the primary audience, because of their exclusivity. Ultimately the strategy may be considered to have backfired, because it was the mobilisation of parents that led to the advert's withdrawal on television – though of course this did attract extra free publicity and the print adverts continued to be run.

Representation

The key representation here is of the brand Reebok but that is inextricably tied up with the depiction of 50 Cent and other cultural icons. In the advert featuring 50 Cent the references to the toughness of his origins and his involvement with violent crime represent him (and the brand?) as tough and macho. His success, as witnessed through his jewels, his pose – slightly furrowed brow, stern expression, head slightly tilted – offers him as ambiguously threatening or heroic. The campaign's slogan is assertive and unapologetic and suggests individualism.

Values and ideology

Building on the representations discussed above, a number of values and ideologies can be seen in evidence:

- Sportswear = fashion.
- Black US culture is stereotyped as violent.
- Street violence is glamorised.
- Reebok = expression of individuality.
- Reebok = precious, ephemeral and desirable.

Institution

The main institutional issue seems to be that of Reebok, positioning itself alongside other sportswear manufacturers as a leisurewear brand, integral to popular culture. The already well-developed link between sportswear manufacturers and black icons is seen in evidence. A further institutional aspect lies in the withdrawal of the 50 Cent television spot after complaints.

Good ways of researching this are to collect press articles about the campaign, information about the complaints it had received, its withdrawal and web-blog commentaries and critiques of it. You can use these to help consider the theories, issues and debates that you might incorporate into a question using this campaign.

Several websites might be of particular use in doing this. The BBC news site is almost unfailingly useful. Start with www.bbc.co.uk then search using keywords for your campaign. They reported on the issue of the glamorisation of gun crime for example. Try searching for 'Is 50 glorifying guns?' Three sites which debate current advertising campaigns that are generating publicity and controversy are www.gig wise.com, www.adrants.com and www.ad-rag.com. The contributors are opinionated and often irreverent, making them an excellent read. Often the entries are extensive and detailed. Ad-rag in particular is a goldmine.

Is 50 glorifying guns?

50 Cent's TV ad for Reebok has been pulled since 54 complaints were made about it.

The I Am What I Am campaign launched a month back and shows 50 in a grimey warehouse, chatting about surviving nine bullets.

Mothers Against Guns wanted Reebok boycotted for glorifying gun culture. They have now praised the company's bravery for pulling the campaign.

Reebok says the ad is positive because it shows 50's life to date and what he's had to overcome to get to where he's at. What do you say?

WHAT YOU'RE SAYING

Is this just the hype the advertisers want? Is 50 a good role model if he's laughing about getting shot?

Thanks for your comments. This debate is now closed. A selection of your emails is published below:

j-zee
It is unfair to say that reebok are using gun crime to sell their kicks this is not the case as 50 and his music is sellin' their trainers and not his violent gun and drugs past.
big up 50 dis' man is on top of his game.
g g g g g g-unit

richard henton
reebok is right, it shows a positive side of 50 of how hes over come his 9 shootings and is here to tell the tale . . .

Jennifer
The problem is 50 Cent, and The Game for that matter, seem to be proud of the fact that they have been shot at several times. They are making a living out of the fact that they used to ride around in gangs where guns where regularly used. The responsible thing for 50 Cent to do (and Reebok) would be to say how stupid it was to get involved

Figure 7: Researching ad campaigns – BBC website on 50 Cent, © BBC

In this instance Ad-rag debated the anomaly in a corporate brand invoking the audience to express their individuality. They expressed a good deal of cynicism about the authenticity of the celebrity quotes.

This could be useful in discussing values and institution. The campaign doesn't neatly fit the AIDA theory and the following article from Ad-rag can help to unpack and debate that.

" adland: Reebok adds more stars to 'I Am What I Am' "

Posted by: caffeinegoddess on Thursday, May 12, 2005 — 04:00 PM CEST

Reebok, known lately as RBK, is **adding more star power** to their **'I Am What I Am'** campaign, created by New York advertising agency **mcgarrybowen**. Monday they announced they will be adding actors Christina Ricci and John Leguizamo, Boston Red Sox pitcher Curt Schilling, and NFL Philadelphia Eagles quarterback Donovan McNabb to their campaign.

The **'I Am What I Am'** is the company's largest advertising spend in nearly a decade. The concept behind the campaign is to encourage young people to embrace their own individuality by celebrating their contemporary heroes including music icons, athletes and entertainers.

'Reebok has definitely struck a chord with our **"I Am What I Am"** brand message,' said Brian Povinelli, Reebok's vice president of global integrated marketing. 'Being aspirational and inspirational is key to the campaign's success. Christina, John, Curt and Donovan have intriguing stories to share and they truly embody our brand attributes of authenticity and individuality.'

The ads give each celebrity the opportunity to break through the fiction that surrounds their public persona.

I think it's walking a funny line because to be an individual, you don't follow the crowd or what the 'hip' kids are doing. And yet this campaign is encouraging folks to follow the rich and famous. And what's individual about the entire NFL wearing Reebok? It was also the point of the **parent group that boycotted**

50 cent's TV ad which eventually went into the ol' bannage bin. Ads that want to talk individuality run the risk of coming off as 'self-important' bologna.

The press release claims 'the ads give each celebrity the opportunity to break through the fiction that surrounds their public persona.' But so much of celebrities fame is based on a fiction that is created by a long line of PR and image folks. Is this something that we can really believe as authentic?

One also has to wonder if they are really direct quotes by the celebs or if they are something crafted by a copywriter. And the same for the copy in the TV spots. Did Iverson really sit down and write that? Somehow I doubt it. It's probably more feasible for them to have said the quotes in the print pieces.

Overall the design of the campaign is great. But it feels as if the quotes just sort of hang there. And in the billboards without the quotes, the ads just become portrait shots with the RBK logo. For those who have seen the TV or the other parts to the campaign it works, but for anyone who doesn't know of the other ads, it says nothing.

One thing I found very interesting, and maybe the best part of the whole sheebang, is that Reebok is going to launch an **online forum** where the average Joe can create their own '**I Am What I Am**' ads. They can also nominate somcone who they feel truly embodies the campaign message. Now that speaks to individuality, probably stronger than the celeb ads.

The campaign broke globally in February and has featured Lucy Liu, Allen Iverson, Kelly Holmes, Jay-Z, Yao Ming, Nicole Vaidisova, 50 Cent, Stevie Williams, and Iker Casillas among others.

Reproduced with kind permission of Jane Goldman, http://ad-rag.com

This material can be applied to an exam question at random – see diagram on page 172 for one example. Here are some suggestions about how this could be worked through:

1 *Break the question down into its key components:*

- standing out from the crowd
- essential part of any advertising campaign

- discuss with detailed reference

- a recent campaign

2 *Work out what's needed to respond to each question element:*

- 'Standing out' . . . this refers to being different, distinctive. This might involve breaking rules, perhaps subverting advertising conventions, conventions of a specific genre or product group perhaps. Also there was the idea of attracting attention, perhaps by courting controversy. 'Standing out' might just mean being the best, excellent in its way.

- 'The crowd' . . . advertising is a saturated market with a great deal of competition for attention. This has created ad fatigue in some, it is argued, perhaps explaining the need for ever more creative ways of capturing and retaining audience attention.

- 'Essential' . . . 'any' . . . these are fairly extreme words and would form the basis for some debate. Think of some exceptions to argue against the question's quote.

- 'Discuss' . . . a reminder to debate the quote.

- 'Detailed' . . . 'recent campaign' defined what was needed in terms of textual examples.

3 *Relate the question demands to the chosen campaign. See the brainstorm on p. 172.*

4 *Consider ways to integrate the key concepts and issues, theories and debates.*

5 *Finally, put the points into some sort of order so that a structured line of argument can develop.*

- *Introduction* – Advertising very crowded. Standing out helps but isn't essential. More important with certain audiences, e.g. young people.

- Also, there are many ways of standing out. Some campaigns might stand out in some ways and conform to convention in others.

- *Main points* – Introduce the Reebok campaign, the market situation, its form and style, the use of 50 Cent.

- Stand out? – be different, catch attention . . . discuss genre conventions, sport versus fashion, product versus brand.

- Notoriety – the withdrawal of the advert. Glamorisation of violence?

- Discuss significance of Audience.

- Representation and Values – 50 Cent, Reebok. The validity of the promotion of individuality (or not).

- Relate this campaign to other sportswear campaigns. Stand out or conventional?

- *Conclusion.* Adverts need to stand out to be successful but equally they need to conform to audience expectations and enhance the public image of the client, reinforcing its core (conservative) values, even when it appears that a more liberal or anarchic message is being conveyed.

Figure 8

BRITISH NEWSPAPERS

It is an obvious thing to say but don't forget to consider the title of this topic – it is easy to overlook it. The focus of this part of the specification is newspapers, as opposed to magazines, that are produced in Great Britain or the United Kingdom. The content section of the specification helps a little further with this definition. It points to 'analysis and evaluation of a range of national newspapers, as well as the local press (including free newspapers) using the Key Concepts'. So that should define for you the topic area that you need to study. Remember also that the title of the paper refers to 'contemporary topics'. This should help you to refine further the focus of your study. As we saw in the Introduction, 'contemporary' is defined as being within the five years prior to your course. Assuming that you have a good idea of what a newspaper is you should have a firm sense of what it is you are looking at for this topic.

So what is it you need to know about British newspapers for this unit. Well, the bullet points in the subject content section of the specification provide further guidance. Here they are:

- Analysis and evaluation of a range of national newspapers, as well as the local press (including free newspapers), using the key concepts

- Analysis and evaluation of press coverage of an issue or story

- Critiques of, and debates around, press coverage (e.g. privacy; sensationalism; inaccuracy and fabrication; propaganda; emphasis upon sex, stars and personalities, etc.). Proposals for reform

- Defences, and positive aspects, of the press

- News and entertainment values of the press

■ Press ideologies (politics and the press; political and social orientation of the press; values implicit in news and feature stories of specific newspapers)

■ Press audiences (circulations; readerships; the press and audiences segmentation; relationships with readers)

The first point offers you the opportunity to focus your attention on a specific aspect of coverage in the press. Notice that the word 'press' implies that you may need to look at a range of newspapers in order to tackle a question based on this aspect. One way you might consider looking at this is to consider the different approaches taken by two or more different newspapers to an issue or story. You need also think through the difference between an issue and a story. 'Issue' implies something rather broader than a story. A story implies a report that relates to a single event. Of course there may be follow-up stories which have been printed subsequent to the initial story. An issue on the other hand might well cover a much broader area, for example the coverage of a matter relating to people's health or how they are treated in hospital. If this is a topic area within British newspapers you are going to revise you need to look in close detail at such an issue or story and collect detailed examples from different newspapers to show how it has been covered.

> **NOTE**
>
> A cuttings file is a really useful tool in revising this topic area. All you need is a scrapbook into which you can paste cuttings of the stories and issues you are monitoring. It is even more useful if you can find time as you go along to annotate these with some short comments to identify what you see as their significance.

CRITIQUES AND DEBATES

For many people this point is the core of any consideration of British newspapers. The tabloids or, more accurately, popular press, often referred to as the red-top newspapers because of the colour of their mastheads, have a reputation for sensational and fabricated stories, which are often heavily celebrity-focused. Ethical considerations of the press inevitably link closely with the third bullet point which looks at the other side of the press, its more positive aspects. Perhaps the best way to see this issue is as a debate. Clearly one positive aspect of the British press is its role within our democracy. The press is often seen as an important defender of our freedom because of the way it is able to keep an eye on governments, large organisations and even individuals who might threaten our well-being and our freedom. Collecting examples of newspaper 'campaigns' on issues that seem to focus on the public interest, for example legislation passed in the European Parliament, is a good starting point for tackling any questions that look at the positive and negative aspects of the British press.

On the other hand there is an argument that says that there should be limits to what the press can do in terms of what it can reveal about people's private lives for example. Commonly stories in the press are branded as exposés, but how far such exposés are public interest is often questionable. The phrase 'in the public interest' is central to the debate. It certainly features heavily in the PCC Code of Conduct which you should check out at www.pcc.org.uk.

> The PCC is the main regulatory body for British newspapers. Its code of conduct is a useful starting point for any work around ethical issues to do with the British press. It basically provides a set of guidelines by which journalists and their editors are supposed to operate in gathering and reporting news. It deals with issues relating to privacy and inaccuracy in some detail.
>
> NOTE

A good starting point might be to consider coverage of the royal family. How far do you think it is in the public interest to reveal details of the private lives of the royals? This is also a good starting point for looking at the issue of celebrity coverage. How far do you think celebrities (called stars and personalities in the specification), most of whom gain their celebrity status through the press, are entitled to protect their own privacy and how far are they fair game for journalists when they go out and starting behaving bizarrely or downright badly? A case study on someone like Kate Moss or Pete Doherty would be ideal here.

Appropriately at this point, you also need to consider the mention in the bullet point of 'emphasis on sex'. Commonly you will hear people in the media say that 'sex sells'. They know that readers all have an interest in this topic, particularly in relation to the sex lives of the rich and famous. Posh and Becks are a prime example of this. Similarly many people would point to the exploitation and fetishisation of women's bodies, particularly in the popular press, as an example of this emphasis on sex. Certainly it can be argued that the representation of women in the popular press has done a good deal to define their role within society and hold back progress to gender equality. The issue of propaganda fits more comfortably under the point relating to press ideologies, so we have dealt with it there (p. 177).

Finally there is the point relating to proposals for reform. This was probably much more of an issue at the end of last century than it is now. Certainly throughout the 1990s there were lots of suggestions for curbing the supposed excesses of the tabloid press. Even confronted with extreme cases of fabrication and sensationalism, such as in the *Mirror*'s publication of fake photographs of British soldiers torturing Iraqi prisoners, few politicians called for greater regulation of the press. One organisation that makes a useful contribution to the debate is the Campaign for Press and Broadcasting Freedom. You should find some useful and up-to-date information on their website, www.cpbf.org.uk.

The point concerned with news and entertainment values presents some interesting challenges. 'News values' is an important concept in studying news media. It refers to the notion that some stories are more important than others and therefore are given greater prominence. A newspaper's front page lead is the most prominent story and consequently the one the editor believes to be the most important. Looking at the front page leads (and to a lesser extent the inside page leads) will tell you a lot about the news values of the newspaper. It is also useful to compare news values across different national titles for any given day. For example, do the 'quality' press, formerly the broadsheets, lead with the same story as the popular press? On some days one story will dominate all newspapers; on other days each will lead with a different story. Try collecting some recent examples of these two occurrences to use as examples in the exam.

'Entertainment values' is rather different, as it is not a concept you are likely to encounter in many textbooks looking at news. What is implied is all the other material in newspapers that is not directly concerned with their fiction of reporting news. You need to look at such things as celebrity gossip, fashion and television coverage. Less obvious items are articles on travel, and broader cultural issues such as books, films and music. A close inspection of both ends of the national newspaper market will reveal that neither the popular nor the 'quality' titles have a monopoly of interest in any of these. Don't make the trite assumption that the popular press is obsessed with celebrity gossip while the 'qualities' care only for opera and ballet. A detailed analysis of a couple of titles should show you that the truth is more complex than that. You may also like to consider that the press uses so much of its editorial space entertaining its readers because it is in a competitive market in which electronic media are able to deliver news to their audiences much more quickly.

Ideology can be a difficult concept to grasp. In essence it means a system of beliefs. The word 'ideology' is used a lot in Media Studies to talk about the values that a media text carries with it either in an open or in a covert way. Press ideologies, therefore, refer to the values and beliefs that a newspaper, or sometimes a group of newspapers, carries. These are not always on the surface and often they will be quite complex, and at times they will seem to be in conflict with one another. To understand the ideology that underpins a newspaper, you need to study it over a period of time. You should look out for recurring themes and ideas within the newspaper at both the choice of stories to cover and the way these are presented. For example, what slant does the newspaper take in its coverage of stories about such issues as the following?

- asylum seekers

- house prices

- European legislation

- drug users

- education.

You might find it useful to take one or more of these issues and monitor the coverage in a couple of different newspapers over the period of a week or so. By doing so, you should learn a lot about the ideology and values of a newspaper and the extent to which it can be argued it is putting out propaganda in favour of one political party.

You should also look out for any evidence of political bias. For example, is there evidence that a newspaper is more supportive of one political party than another? This may be evident in both its choice and presentation of stories that show a particular party in a positive light and negative stories about another party. Of course it may not necessarily be consistent in doing these things for a number of reasons, not least to create at least the impression that it is impartial and objective in its coverage of national and international events. Certainly one change that has occurred is that newspapers are far less predictable in their political allegiances. This is in part due to the change within the political landscape itself with both main parties battling much more for the centre ground of politics rather than the extremes.

Finally, as you can see, you need to go into the exam room equipped with some information about the readers of newspapers. Finding out circulation figures is reasonably straightforward. The Audit Bureau of Circulation website (http://www. abc.org.uk) carries figures for national newspaper distribution while the Joint Industry Committee for Regional Newspaper Research (http://jiab.jicreg.co.uk/ index.cfm) provides some interesting detail about the provincial press, not least a useful breakdown offering a demographic of the readership of most provincial free and paid-for titles. Perhaps the interesting detail in terms of circulation figures is the tendency in recent years for newspaper circulation to decline. This is often seen as part of a more general decline in mass audiences as people find other ways of filling their leisure time and finding information in preference to reading newspapers and watching television. Certainly you might like to consider what are the main sources of competition to newspapers – for example websites providing news of different types, and 24-hour news channels on digital television. You should also consider how newspapers have responded to this competition through marketing strategies such as free offers and competitions as well as some of the other strategies you will have considered.

You will have noticed that much of the focus in looking at the bullet points in the specification is on national newspapers. That is perhaps inevitable given that many of the major debates about the press are the primary concern of the national press, particularly the popular press in terms of issues such as ethics and sensationalism as well as political and ideological bias. The local press is, however, an equally valid area of study particularly in terms of issues relating to readership, news and entertainment values and some of the positive aspects of the press, especially in terms of their value to local communities.

So, to sum up, the content of this unit implies that you have to:

- Study a range of newspapers including local and national titles.
- Monitor and analyse how they cover a story or issue.
- Consider the positive and negative aspects of the press.
- Be aware of the news and entertainment values behind press coverage.
- Be aware of newspapers' ideological and political allegiances.
- Be informed about their circulation and readership.

KEY CONCEPTS: HOW DO THEY RELATE TO THIS TOPIC?

Of course as you will have discovered in our introduction to MED2, all of these points have to be allied to the key concepts, which serve to underpin all of your study in this and other topics. Clearly some of the areas you need to explore as part of the key concepts will overlap quite heavily with the subject content. So it is a good idea to work through each of the key concept areas to determine what additional investigation they imply in your study of this topic.

The concept of Audience for example will be covered to a large degree by the final bullet point on p. 174. You must realise, however, that despite the big overlap there are also areas implied by audience as a key concept that you must also pay attention to.

Representation

This is quite a large issue in terms of British newspapers and you should realise that it is central to any study that you might make of ideological issues in the press. The key concept as defined in the specification invites you to look at who is represented, by whom, how and why they are represented in this way. You can link this readily to any study you might have made of a minority group with the British press for example. Representations are value-laden and inevitably reveal an ideological perspective implicit in the newspaper's reporting of events. Of course the overwhelming question relates to the fairness and accuracy of the representation. This question is extremely difficult to answer. One way of having a stab at it is to choose a group of people or an issue that you are familiar with, teenagers or football fans for example, and try to match your experiences and understanding of such a group with that represented in a newspaper.

Media languages and forms

A quick skim through the bullet points for this key concept will reveal fairly quickly that few of them relate directly to this topic. Most are in fact linked rather unhelpfully to a study of moving-image texts such as film and television. You can, however, usefully relate some of the ideas to the still images that dominate the press, generally in the form of photographs. Certainly issues of denotation and connotation and the significance of these connotations can be explored through looking in detail at press photographs. This is a particularly valuable exercise when you apply some of the skills you have developed for the MED1 exam and consider how captions are used to anchor the meanings available within the photographic images. You may also want to link this back to issues of representation. For example how are press illustrations, including graphic material such as cartoons, used to represent figures in the news? You may also find it useful to give consideration to how press photographs come about. This is often revealed by looking at the detail within the photograph, or the mise en scène. Many press photographs are carefully posed to create a specific effect. Others you may find are taken more spontaneously. These include paparazzi photographs often taken without the subject being aware of the presence of the photographer.

Narrative

There are two different types of narrative that you need to be especially aware of in exploring newspapers. The first is quite obviously the way in which narrative is used to construct individual stories within the newspaper. The second concerns more the construction of the newspaper as a whole. For the first type of narrative you should consider some of the elements of media language that might be usefully included above – for example how headlines, typographic devices and illustrations are used to construct a newspaper story. Note for example how the first paragraph or intro is made to stand out from the rest of the story. Look at how the story is made to flow, taking the reader through the key details from beginning to end. Think too about the importance of conflict in narrative. Most newspaper stories focus on some type of conflict, be it between rival politicians or rival football managers. Consider how character is used to develop the conflict within the narrative. Think how far the reader is encouraged to take one side or another within this conflict. Again there is an important issue of both representation and ideology at work here. On a simple level this is an issue of identification noticeable for example in stories where the United Kingdom is in conflict with a foreign power, be it war or football.

Narrative is also a usual mechanism for looking at how a newspaper is constructed as a whole. Narrative is a means of controlling the flow of information in a text, and a newspaper is put together in such a way that information is given to the reader in an organised and controlled manner. You may notice that most newspapers are constructed in a similar way. Whatever paper you are reading, you will expect to find certain information in certain places, sport on the back pages for example.

As you can see there is quite a lot of ground to cover if you are going to prepare for all the possible questions on British newspapers that MED2 might throw at you. Of course you may choose to gamble on the basis of your research into questions that have been set recently and those that you think are 'due for an outing'. But taking such a risk is really appropriate only if you have not been focused on your studies and have left revision to the very last minute. In such a circumstance being able to answer something is better than being able to answer nothing. Inevitably you may feel better prepared to deal with certain topics than others and this feeling might usefully inform your decision about which question in the pair on the exam paper you choose to have a go at.

One really important issue we need to address before you do anything more is that of exemplification. Exemplification is a rather grandiose term for giving examples. As we have suggested to you previously, a good AS answer will support any argument or assertion with appropriate examples. MED2 as we have seen tells you on the front of the paper that you must do this. For British newspapers then you need to have ready a series of possible examples to use to support your answer. This is a good point at which to check back over the subject content and the key concepts to make a list of the kinds of examples that might come in especially useful. When you have done this you are likely to come up with a list similar to the one below:

- Story – construction, narrative, point of view

- Issue – coverage

- Sensationalism, fabricated story, celebrity gossip

- Press exposing wrongdoing or campaigns

- News agenda, e.g. prioritising of news

- Issues of representation and stereotyping

- Political and ideological bias in the press

- Evidence of relationship with readers, e.g. opportunities for feedback or participation. Segmentation of readership within an edition, e.g. women's pages, racing pages, financial pages.

Ideally the examples you have chosen will form part of a cuttings file that enables you to have ready at hand good contemporary examples of texts that you can use to support the arguments you wish to make. You need to take a run at this, ensuring you look at a range of newspapers from which to select your examples. It is also a good idea to consider the coverage of a story or issue across at least two newspapers. This should give you a useful point of comparison in a number of ways. Firstly, how a story or issue is covered. Secondly, some sense of the ideological positioning of different newspapers in terms of the attitudes and values that they display. Thirdly, it provides an opportunity for you to consider how each of the texts addresses its readers. All three of these uses of an example could well prove valuable in the exam regardless of the type of question that you choose to answer.

This is a good opportunity to consider some of the decisions you will have to make when you get into the exam room itself and are confronted by the questions on British Newspapers. Look first at the pair of questions below. They are taken from the January 2005 paper.

EXAM QUESTION

(a) 'Tabloids spread moral panics (. . .) Some campaigns, for example the anti-asylum seekers campaign, have been misinformed by hatred and exaggeration which has played on people's fears and prejudices.' (Roy Greenslade in the *Guardian* Media Supplement, 3 February 2003.)

Is such criticism fair? Support your argument with examples.

AQA 2005

Many students are put off by 'long' questions, for example ones that run to three or four lines or more on an exam paper. Even more are put off when they see a quotation, especially if it is one they have never seen before or it is attributed to someone they have never heard of. Our advice is don't be put off so easily. It doesn't matter if you don't know the quote, it is unlikely that you will most of the time. What does matter is that you are prepared to read the quote carefully, and re-read it if necessary until you have a good idea what it is getting at. In many questions, although the quote is helpful, it may not be absolutely central to the question; that is to say you may well be able to tackle the question without fully grasping the quote. This is not the case with this question. You must understand that Roy Greenslade is attacking the tabloids, or popular press, for creating moral panics. You should have come across the term 'moral panic' in your study of this topic and know that it refers to the idea of the media stirring up public concern over a specific issue. You should also know that some sections of the popular press like to foster resentment towards certain groups such as asylum seekers by running campaigns that play on people's fears.

The question you have to answer is whether such a criticism is fair. You are also told to support your argument with examples. Of course, by this stage in your education, you should realise that there is no right or wrong answer to this question. You are not being tested on your ability to say yes it is or no it isn't. What you are being asked to do is to offer an argument saying that tabloids do spread moral panics, or that no they don't or that (most likely) sometimes they do but much of the time they don't.

EXAM QUESTION

(b): News can be presented very differently in different newspapers.

Discuss the reasons for this, giving detailed examples from at least two newspapers.

AQA 2005

Certainly on the surface this seems a much more straightforward question. Indeed one of the problems that the question poses is that what it states is so blindingly obvious that you may think there is some sub-text or hidden agenda that you have missed. The potential difficulty that the question poses, however, is its very breadth. Other than the direction to look at two newspapers as a minimum, we seem to be left with a pretty blank canvas here. We might compare for example:

- popular with 'quality'
- local with national
- daily with Sunday

Or we might even compare two newspapers appealing to a similar target audience, the *Mirror* and the *Sun* for example.

Try to see this kind of choice as an opportunity rather than as a grim decision.

Let's have a look at another pair of questions on the topic of British Newspapers. Here are the options from the June 2005 MED2 paper.

EXAM QUESTION

(a) How well does your local newspaper serve the interests of the people in your local area?

Support your views with detailed reference to stories and features you have studied.

(b) Media publicist, Max Clifford, described the British Press as being the most savage in the world.

How far do you agree with this view of British newspapers? Give examples of news stories and features to support your opinion.

AQA 2005

No need by now to remind you of the importance of reading both questions carefully before making a decision. Obviously your response to this pair is going to be largely determined by the texts that you have studied. Certainly if the focus of your study for this unit has been the narrow confines of the local press, then question (a) is more likely to fit in with your preparation than (b). However, if you have prepared properly for the exam, you should be in a position to tackle either question, so take some time to consider which of the two is better for you. Let's take a close look at the options.

Question (a) is about local newspapers. It is about their role and function in relation to their audience. It is also a question that asks you how effectively they perform this role, so you are being asked for some element of opinion in this question.

Note also you are being asked in this question to provide evidence from the texts you have studied. This ability to use evidence from texts to support your argument is more important in many respects than the actual argument that you put forward. Demonstrating close knowledge of the style and content of your local newspaper is the key thing here. Don't forget though that it is your ability to analyse these features of the local paper that matters here. A question like this has one great big trapdoor waiting for students – be sure to avoid it. You can do so by simply making sure that you do not end up describing the contents of your newspaper. Remember the best students can tell you why, not just what. So a question like this needs you to be able to rehearse ideas about why certain stories and features appear in local newspapers.

As soon as you see questions like this, you should feel obliged to start making a list. In this case it is a list of features that you can expect in your local newspaper. You should start like this:

- Local news
- Local sport
- Letters to the editor
- Local entertainment

Now think about the audience for a local newspaper. Unlike a national title, local newspapers rarely have a clearly defined demographic in terms of age, gender and social class. Their readership is defined geographically in terms of the circulation area that they serve. This fact offers you a potentially interesting way in to this question. How does the newspaper you have studied try to appeal to this broad section of the population? Does it for example have the same appeal to old people as it does to teenagers? The answer may well be that it tries. How far it succeeds might well form the basis of a good response this question. So perhaps another list of different groups, such as teenagers and retired people, might also help your planning of this essay.

Local newspapers are often seen as rather bland, tamely reporting local events without ever appearing critical of local organisations such as councils. Some are seen to do little more than rewrite press releases. Certainly this accusation can be levelled at many of the free-sheets now in circulation. Many do little more than offer minimal editorial coverage to fill space left by advertisers. This is not always the case. Many local newspapers campaign vigorously on behalf of local issues. Try to find any examples in your local newspaper that might serve as an example of this.

> **NOTE**
>
> The word 'features' in this essay title is a little ambivalent. Here it is likely that it is used in the technical sense of an editorial item that offers information which is not really hard news. Features often provide an opportunity for a journalist to write in depth about an issue and provide interesting background detail. In lay terms a feature also means a characteristic which might include all of the non-news items found in a newspaper. Try making a list of both sorts of 'feature' you have found in a recent edition of your local newspaper.

The second question, (b), offers us a statement by Max Clifford, described as a media publicist. It helps if you know who Max Clifford is, particularly in terms of how he operates in relation to the press by selling stories and representing the interests of controversial figures. If you don't know about Max Clifford the question should still be accessible to you.

He is describing the British press as the most savage in the world. This implies that the British Press is vicious and uncompromising in the way in which it depicts individuals in the stories it covers. The phrase 'in the world' seems to imply that you need to make a comparison with newspapers from other countries. Realistically this is not the case. Not only does the second sentence invite you to focus on 'this view of British newspapers', the title of the section is British Newspapers. It would be unfair of the examiner to ask for your knowledge of foreign press in this context.

> **NOTE**
>
> Never be put off a question because it names or quotes a person you have not come across. Examiners like to use quotes in questions as they think it helps add substance and credibility to what they are asking. Questions should be self-contained and you should be able to answer them regardless of any names. So read the question carefully to make sure you understand what is being asked and forget the name.

Notice this question is another 'how far do you agree?'. Any response from 'not at all' to 'completely' is possible.

Again be wary of the trapdoor. Don't just write down a list of all the examples you have collected of press savagery towards individuals. You might like to start with a distinction between the popular and 'quality' press. Certainly the popular news-papers are more concerned with 'personality', especially in relation to celebrity. This is where much of the 'savagery' is to be found.

It would be helpful if you could start by offering some sense of what you understand by the word 'savage'. This will help you define how you intend to approach the essay. 'Savage' clearly carries with it connotations of behaving in a way that is not civilised or appropriate. It also has connotation of making vicious attacks, presumably on people.

> **NOTE**
>
> It would certainly be useful when approaching a question of this type to be able to offer some factual information about the factors that might limit what the press can say and do. You need to be able to show at the very least that you know about the libel laws and the role of the PCC in curbing the excesses of the press and offering redress to those it may have wrongly savaged.

In essence there is a debate at the heart of a question of this type. That debate surrounds the ideas of freedom and responsibility in relation to newspapers. Clearly a free press able to expose those who seemingly do wrong in our society is an important aspect of democracy. Similarly the need for the press to act responsibly and not abuse its great power is important in terms of our individual freedom.

Of course a simple statement like that begs for further clarification and definition. What do we mean by 'wrong'? What do we mean by 'responsibly'? Well as we have already indicated, it is not your job to come up with chapter and verse on this one. Maybe a few years down the line when you are doing your doctoral thesis on some aspect of the press, then maybe. For the time being what is expected of you is to show that you have at least some awareness of the issues involved here. Put simply, that you are able to indicate that there is something that needs to be debated rather than to see this as an opportunity to rant on about the press coverage of one of your favourite personalities. Don't forget that the debate has to be supported with evidence you have gathered from some recent examples of press coverage which you have already prepared in readiness for a question of this type. In fact the essence of a good response to this type of question lies in selecting appropriate and convincing examples.

PART 4

CONCLUSION

188 CONCLUSION

We hope that you have found this book useful and that you will feel able to go into your AS Media Studies exams feeling a little bit more confident than you did before you read it. The advice that we offer comes from many years of teaching and examining Media Studies, so we very much hope that you will act upon it. We also hope that it will help you to get a better grade.

More importantly we hope that this book has stimulated your interest in Media Studies. The texts you are studying for your exams were designed to offer pleasure to their audiences. Don't forget that. Studying the media should in itself be a pleasurable experience despite the many nights of hard revision that you have subjected yourself to.

Just studying for an exam does not mean that you can't enjoy the texts you are working with. Indeed one school of thought would argue that the close critical scrutiny to which you have subjected the texts should enhance the pleasure you get from them. Perhaps so close to the exam, it might be a little bit difficult to persuade you of the validity of this argument. Maybe, however, you will reflect on this later and acknowledge that studying for the AS exams has been an enriching experience for you.

Certainly one thing we would suggest is that, if this book has fuelled your enthusiasm for the subject, then you should make this enthusiasm evident when you are writing your exams. Nothing pleases examiners more than students who write with genuine enthusiasm and energy in their exams. We also hope that you may have been inspired to take your study of the media further, at least to have a go at the A2 course and perhaps even through to undergraduate level.

Whatever path you choose – good luck.

PART 5

APPENDICES

SAMPLE AQA MATERIALS

SAMPLE FRONT PAGE OF THE AQA AS MEDIA STUDIES MED2 EXAMINATION

Note the word 'textual' – it's all about texts and don't forget it! It's about 'contemporary' and don't forget it – unless of course you are doing the documentary question in which case remember some historical examples as well!

General Certificate of Education
January 2005
Advanced Subsidiary Examination

AQA
ASSESSMENT and
QUALIFICATIONS
ALLIANCE

Write all your rough notes in the book and cross them through so they don't get marked inadvertently. If you need more paper – ask and make sure you put your details on it (name, centre number, candidate number) and fix it to the answer book.

MEDIA STUDIES   **MED2**
Unit 2   **Textual Topics in Contemporary Media**

Monday 17 January 2005   Afternoon Session

Date is published . . . in advance. Find out exactly when the afternoon session is – you may have two papers back to back – if you're lucky!

In addition to this paper you will require:
an 8-page answer book.

Time allowed: 1 hour 30 minutes

So about 40 minutes a question.

Not one, not three, not four . . . two! And each one has to be from a different section. Got it?

No marks for this unfortunately!

Don't forget a spare one!

Instructions
- Use blue or black ink or ball-point pen.
- Write the information required on the front of your answer book. The *Examining Body* for this paper is AQA. The *Paper Reference* is MED2.
- Answer **two** questions, each from a different topic area.

This is a simplified version of the assessment objectives. It's written so that you will understand it.

So spend an equal amount of time on each.

Information
- The maximum mark for this paper is 60. All questions carry 30 marks.
- In this paper you will be expected to:
  – show what you know about media texts and topics using the **Key Concepts**
  – comment on media theories, ideas, debates and information.
- You will be rewarded for specific reference to contemporary media texts.
- You are reminded of the need for good English and clear presentation. Your answers should be in continuous prose. Quality of written communication will be assessed.

Could be it's important!

I.e. show us you have done a Media Studies course and you know about these things.

So make sure you mention texts and make sure they are contemporary – unless you are doing documentary of course.

Check your English at the end. Put right any obvious errors in spelling, punctuation and grammar.

Presentation is important as is clear writing, good use of paragraph structure

So don't try blank verse or notes!

You will be marked on your written communication – not your English but your ability to write effectively and to put together well-structured arguments.

SAMPLE FROM THE MARK SCHEME FOR THE AQA AS MEDIA STUDIES MED2 EXAMINATION

Unit 2: Textual Topics in Contemporary Media: Question 1 a)   (*30 marks*)

Account for the similarities you have found in the techniques used to tell stories by those who make film and broadcast fiction.

Give textual illustration from film AND/OR broadcast fiction texts to support your argument.

Level 6 (26–30 marks)

The answer shows a confident conceptual exploration with a well-developed discussion and a thorough knowledge of the chosen techniques, provides relevant exemplification and demonstrates a clear understanding of how moving image techniques are similar. It shows a critical understanding of relevant ideas, theories, debates or information, confident evaluation and personal response and competent use of appropriate terminology.

Level 5 (21–25 marks)

The answer shows a focused discussion using the conceptual framework and a sound knowledge of the chosen techniques, provides relevant exemplification and demonstrates satisfactory understanding of how moving image techniques are similar. It shows an engaged personal response, sound understanding of relevant ideas, theories, debates or information and an adequate use of appropriate terminology.

'confident conceptual exploration' – You can sound confident by showing you know what you are talking about. This is especially evident in using the correct terminology appropriately and showing good knowledge of the key concepts, which also covers the idea of a 'conceptual exploration'.

'demonstrates a clear understanding' – Shows you really have engaged in the nature of narrative in film and/or broadcast fiction texts.

'critical understanding of relevant ideas, theories, debates or information' – In short you know what media studies is all about and you can talk about texts from an informed critical perspective.

'competent use of appropriate terminology' – You can use the language of Media Studies in a convincing and correct manner.

'well developed discussion' – Suggests you're seeing this question as an opportunity to consider in detail the narrative techniques in the question.

'personal response' – It's about you and what you think, not what your teacher has told you to think!

'confident evaluation' – I.e. you can make your own critical judgements and support them.

EXTRACT FROM THE AQA REPORT ON THE MEDIA STUDIES EXAMINATION (GCE 2005, JANUARY SERIES)

Unit One – Reading the Media (MED1)

This January there was yet another increase in the number of candidates sitting the MED1 examination. 5541 candidates produced an analysis of the first three minutes of an episode of *My Wife and Kids* broadcast on 2 November 2003 on Trouble Re-Loaded.

Yet again it is pleasing to report that the good practice commented upon in Reports on the Examination in previous years continues to take place. There is certainly growing evidence to suggest that most centres, and indeed candidates, recognise more and more that this examination is designed to encourage an individual response to an unseen media text. However, there are still a few centres where candidates seem to have been taught an 'ideal' essay structure based around a supposed ideal approach. Although this might be because the nature of the unseen text just happens to be one that candidates have studied in their centre, it does mean that there are still some examiners who feel as though they are reading virtually the same essay from all candidates. Sometimes the only possible means of differentiation is by prose style. Candidates should be assured that there is *not* a mark scheme that is set in stone. Examiners are asked to look for readings that are genuinely grounded in a knowledge and understanding of the Media Key Concepts and that display some sense of independent thought and evidence of critical autonomy. Whilst it is recognised that there is a need for a sense of logical structure to an essay, a universal template does tend to disadvantage candidates.

> Clear indication that you have the freedom to explore ideas as long as these are linked to the key concepts.

The text in question this examination series was the first three minutes of a typical sit-com broadcast on a niche digital channel available on satellite and cable TV. There was a wealth of material for candidates to deal with. The text was chosen because it was considered particularly suitable for a reading using the main Key Concepts, but also likely to be one which many candidates would be familiar (especially since the programme is now also transmitted on BBC2) thereby, hopefully, making the examination a particularly pertinent one for them. The advantage of video, as noted before in previous examinations, is that candidates tend not to fall back on the time-wasting denotative response but are pushed to analyse and evaluate, because they do not have the text in front of them the whole time. It was impressive that so many candidates managed to select from the three-minute sequence the aspects that they considered important and relevant to their own reading and then use their selection to provide an analysis.

> Again candidates are really encouraged to identify what they consider important and not to write to some wretched template given to them by their teacher.

Subject knowledge was frequently sound, with some effective use of learnt terminology and theory (where appropriate), and there was far less of a tendency to jot down as much learning as possible into the answer without really thinking about it. However, there are still some candidates who treat the unseen examination as an opportunity to download as much 'learnt material' as possible, irrespective, it seems at times, of the relevance of such material or indeed their understanding of it. However, in the majority of cases, it was pleasing that, although the question requires that Media Language, Representation and Audience should primarily be examined, many candidates were confident enough to investigate the rather more difficult areas of Institutions and Values and Ideology and these were on the whole also covered well. Indeed there were many more instances of candidates feeling sufficiently confident in their approach to the text that they investigated very fully one or two particular concept areas in great detail and with sophistication and a sense of critical autonomy.

There were of course some common errors. It is still assumed by some candidates that the audience for any media text is represented by whoever seems to appear within the text. Some candidates still try to place a media audience into some kind of age and class grouping that sometimes may be quite arbitrary and self-contradictory.

However, in this examination series the incidences of this approach were far less common than in the past. This might well be because most candidates are in fact the audience for the programme but it was clear that many candidates were fully aware of the secondary audiences as well.

Generally speaking, most candidates treated Media Language with confidence and considerable depth. Media Representations and Audiences were also treated well. It was particularly interesting to note how many candidates were confident enough to discuss matters relating to Values and Ideologies as well. All in all examiners felt that both teachers and candidates are comfortable with the nature of the examination and the responses overall suggested that some excellent teaching and learning is taking place throughout the country.

The following comments are made by Key Concept:

Media Language

The majority of candidates immediately recognised the text as a sit-com, though it was notable that a few candidates thought it was a soap and others simply stated that it belonged to the comedy genre. The great majority of candidates were obviously well aware of the codes and conventions of the situation comedy and were also conversant with the many other similar sit-coms on the television, now and indeed in the past. This meant that references were made to the similarities with, for instance, *My Family* and other contemporary sit-coms. Many candidates were also familiar with other sit-coms that have featured black families such as *The Cosby Show* and *Fresh Prince of Bel-Air*. There was much analysis of the mise-en-scène, though at times it was perhaps pushed to extremes. Whilst, for instance, the opening shot of the exterior of the house and the passing white SUV does suggest a family who are fairly well off and living in suburbia, it is stretching things a little to suggest that the white *sans serif* lettering of the titles suggests binary opposites and racial tensions to come later on in the programme. There was an increased awareness of such things as non-diegetic sound and laughter added later on in the post-production process to help a television audience join in the general ambience. Stock sit-com figures were analysed and there was also much analysis of the narrative structure and the way in which, during the three-minute sequence, several enigmas were posed that would develop the narrative through the episode. However, overall the nature of the Media Language used tended to be treated in a very matter-of-fact manner. Candidates seemed much more interested in looking at the other Key Concepts, which is commendable.

Representation

This was the area that really engaged the interest of almost all candidates. Gender stereotypes were examined with considerable relish and the ambiguities of the characters and their relationships with one another were developed in many interesting ways. Who, for instance, was in charge? The wife never sat down and organised everyone, including her husband, obviously cared for the children and consequently was considered a nurturing mother. The husband clearly misunderstood his eldest daughter and was put out by the superior knowledge of his son. His failing eyesight suggested a man clearly past his prime. Conversely it was argued that the father had everyone running around him while he sat at the table and read his newspaper in true patriarchal style. The three children were examined as three stereotypical characters – the moody/sulky teenage girl, the know-it-all teenage son and the young girl who never wants to grow up.

Similarly the representation of race was handled equally well by most candidates. Many candidates had some sense of the historical background concerning blacks in America and also the ever-increasing number of black stars and producers in Hollywood and American television today. Damon Wayans was recognised by most candidates, as was the historical precedents with programmes like *The Cosby Show* etc. Many candidates has extensive knowledge of all the other black American shows that currently exist on many of the teenage orientated channels on digital television today.

Stronger candidates also examined the nature of the family.

Much was written about the 'perfect nuclear family' and the underlying values implicit in the programme. There was also mention of the American Dream in many responses and how the fact that the black family in this particular programme were so obviously middle-class said much about the values and ideologies implicit in broadcasting, particularly in America.

Audiences

As mentioned above this was an area that was handled far better than before. Instead of attempting to fit media audiences into tight socio-economic groupings, as has happened in previous MED1 examinations, candidates thought more carefully about the likely audience for the programme in terms of content, where it was shown and also when it was shown. So the fact that Trouble is a digital channel, available on Sky and cable, the programme was shown on a Sunday morning, that it was about a family (and a black American family) and that the content of the programme was essentially humorous all tended to inform the candidates' responses in terms of the likely Media Audience. Equally pleasing was the fact that many candidates were aware of the fact that although the primary audience is teenagers, so too there is a possibility that many other audience types may well have been watching (based on the facts stated above) and that this secondary audience is of importance too.

It was evident that the great majority of candidates knew the programme well and were fans. Normally this means that the responses can become quite subjective and based on personal prejudice, but this seemed rarely to be the case in this instance.

Values and Ideology/Institutions

Most candidates had some knowledge of Trouble TV and its sister channel Trouble Re-Loaded and a considerable amount of knowledge about the implications of satellite and cable television in terms of audiences and economics. Most candidates, even if they do not actually own anything other than terrestrial television, seemed to have access in one way or another to satellite/cable television. Very few candidates came to the examination never having watched satellite or cable television. Most candidates seemed to have considerable knowledge of Trouble and all the other niche kids/teenage channels that exist on digital television.

Most candidates were eager to discuss, in varying degrees of sophistication, the values and ideology inherent to the text. As has been alluded to above, this involved the racial issues inherent in a sit-com that would have been unlikely to have been made a couple of decades ago. Many candidates had obviously studied the sit-com and were aware of the impact made by *The Cosby Show* and its legacy today. Several candidates also discussed the nature of the nuclear family and there was also evidence that the work of Chomsky and others had been looked at by several centres as their candidates examined hegemony and the role of media institutions in preserving the status quo.

The examination this winter seems to have stimulated the vast majority of candidates into providing responses that were really very pleasing. There was increasing evidence of a cohort who were well prepared but also confident enough to produce responses that challenged the text and showed genuine evidence of critical thought.

Unit Two – Textual Topics in Contemporary Media (MED2)

There were 1799 candidates entered for this unit. It appeared that some candidates entered had a wider knowledge and a more confident understanding of only one of the topics they chose to write on, perhaps due to the short amount of time between the start of the AS course and the January examination. However, there were some very strong candidates who demonstrated a very solid knowledge of their chosen textual topics and were able to write two balanced answers.

Writing two essays in one and a half hours is a skill which needs practice and it was clear that, at this early stage in the course, it was a skill that some candidates had not yet developed. Some candidates would have benefited from more practice in producing concise, question-focused responses which combined textual knowledge and conceptual understanding with topic related ideas and debates.

The majority of centres seemed to have understood the nature of contemporary as it applies to this unit, namely a text produced within the last five years. Examiners were impressed by the wealth of very recent examples from Film, Television, Documentary, Advertising and British newspaper texts. It needs to be repeated once again that *Psycho* is unacceptable as a key text for this unit and centres are reminded that *Pulp Fiction* is 10 years old. Contemporary texts that candidates have consumed first hand inspire better analysis and engagement with the textual topic; it is only in the Documentary option that historical contextualisation is specified.

> Don't forget this. Contemporary = produced within last five years!

Textual examples are needed for all topics and all questions on this paper with the amount of detail required being signalled in the wording of each question. Strong answers provided plentiful evidence of close study of texts, while weaker ones were generalised and provided hypothetical examples. Candidates should be advised to read questions carefully and be prepared to adapt their textual knowledge and topic understanding in an appropriate way to focus on the set question and always to demonstrate thorough knowledge of the text itself.

> Therefore you have in a nutshell how to prepare for MED2 – get some good textual examples and adapt these to focus on the question. Easy!

There was a noticeable improvement in the application of the conceptual framework to the texts and topics discussed and this was present in answers at all levels. There were still, however, a number of responses which, ignoring the media conceptual framework, consisted primarily of descriptive accounts of media texts, such as the story of a film or a simple factual account of an advertising campaign. Centres are reminded that the application of the Key Concepts is equally important across all four topics in this unit. The majority of candidates showed awareness of this major assessment objective in answers on Film and Broadcast Fiction, discussing their chosen texts in terms of media language, representations and audience and, indeed in stronger answers, values and ideology and institution. It was less apparent in the other three topics on the paper, where some candidates prioritised knowledge of topic information and debates over the evaluation of the texts themselves.

The trend of improvement continues in terms of candidates' knowledge and application of topic area information, ideas and debates. The appropriate use of terminology was particularly strong in the Documentary and Advertising and Marketing topics and there was a pleasing use of technical vocabulary in the Film and Broadcast Fiction area. Examiners commented on the confident use of theory within many candidates' responses and it was pleasing to see answers in which appropriate theories were used confidently to evaluate texts and build up an argument. Media theory was employed to good effect by a growing number of candidates; in many cases appropriate theories were used confidently to evaluate texts and build up an argument. However it must be re-stated that theory led answers are not usually successful for this unit. The major assessment objective (A01) calls for the conceptual approach to texts, parts of texts and the topics themselves; A03(i) counts for fewer marks here and is more important for A2 units.

DOCUMENTARY

EXAMPLE OF A COMPLETED GRID (SEE P. 111)

TECHNIQUE	ISSUE	DEBATE
Selection/compression	Not whole truth. Somone selecting what's important and what's not. Who? Preferred readings. Bias	But . . . otherwise docs would be boring, shapeless, undramatic
Editing	Selection, omission, re-ordering	See above, gives pace, tempo, drama . . .
Use of narrative	Shapes otherwise formless material. Manipulation bias . . .	Gives meaning, form Generates drama, hooks . . .
Relation of sound to image	These may be seamless. Suggest authenticity, truth . . .	Video and audio track may be split. Music heightens emotion. Use of SFX. Realism?
Function of narrator	Explains = accessible	Bias? Preferred readings.
Set-ups	Detracts from notions of actuality/realism	Sometimes necessary if a point is to be clear
Effect of camera/crew	Audience awareness of this. Creates reflexivity	Disrupts notions of actuality and realism
Entertainment	Not documentary's chief aim	Commercial climate
Functions	Inform/educate more important	Ratings important. Documentaries can be fun too

ADVERTISING

EXAMPLE OF A COMPLETED GRID (SEE P. 146)

ADVERTISING: EFFECTS ON MEDIA CONTENT		
Area of debate	**Pro**	**Con**
Financial	Pays for many texts which wouldn't otherwise exist	Exerts an influence over programmes' editorial content in an attempt to attract advertisers and keep them on board. The need to attract high ratings or sales affects their ability to take risks and be experimental
Ethical	Advertisers tend to be fairly conservative and this could be seen as a form of censorship. A relatively high level of regulation in UK prevents pernicious erosion of ethics	Public service ethics of UK broadcasters are eclipsed by greater competition and the need to respond to commercial imperatives. Digital advances seem to take no account of ethical considerations, e.g. endless streams of US cartoons on kids' channels. The responsibility to manage viewing is placed squarely on the audience rather than the broadcaster, as with terrestrial provision
Professional	Advertisers exert a moderating influence because of their desire to increase and protect profit. Don't want to cause offence because of negative PR. The desire of advertisers to reach specific audiences can lead to an improvement in quality, e.g. sport on Sky	Advertising is often blamed for a lack of professional ethics, e.g. deliberate breaches of the ASA code in order to acquire free publicity. Some say 'quality' TV has been 'dumbed down' to haul in larger, more passive audiences for advertisers

ADVERTISING: EFFECTS ON MEDIA CONTENT		
Area of debate	**Pro**	**Con**
Public Service	Commercial imperatives are at work, even in public service organisations like BBC. Some argue that advertising would protect the BBC's public service remit in the longer term. C4?	Usually it's argued that public service is diametrically opposed to the commercial imperative in broadcasting. As such advertising can be seen to threaten public service aims
Audience	Advertising revenue allows for a wide range of programming, esp. on digital channels. Advertising provides the luxury of programming for very niche audiences. Advertising gives the audience more power, with programmes tailored to what they want. It opens up the possibility of a more democratic, less patrician type of broadcasting.	Is it really a wider range of programmes or just more of the same? Programmes more formulaic, less risk-taking. Audiences are bombarded with adverts, esp. a concern with younger viewers perhaps. Advertising creates the illusion of audience power – really hegemony is being reinforced 'by the back door'

Related titles from Routledge

Media Studies: The Essential Resource
Edited by Philip Rayner, Peter Wall and Stephen Kruger

A unique collection of resources for all those studying the media at university and pre-university level, this book brings together a wide array of material including advertisements, political cartoons and academic articles, with supporting commentary and explanation to clarify their importance to Media Studies. In addition, activities and further reading and research are suggested to help kick start students' autonomy. The book is organized around three main sections: Reading the Media, Audiences and Institutions and is edited by the same teachers and examiners who brought us the hugely successful *AS Media Studies: The Essential Introduction.*

This is an ideal companion or standalone sourcebook to help students engage critically with media texts – its key features include:

- further reading suggestions
- a comprehensive bibliography
- a list of web resources.

ISBN10: 0-415-29172-0 (hbk)
ISBN10: 0-415-29173-9 (pbk)

ISBN13: 9-78-0-415-29172-9 (hbk)
ISBN13: 9-78-0-415-29173-6 (pbk)

Available at all good bookshops
For ordering and further information please visit:
www.routledge.com

Related titles from Routledge

A2 Media Studies: The Essential Introduction
by Peter Bennett, Jerry Slater and Peter Wall

A2 Media Studies: The Essential Introduction builds on the work covered by the AS Media Studies syllabus; designed to aid students with the transition from a focus on textual analysis to the consideration of the wider contexts that inform any study of the media. Carefully tailored to the A2 Media Studies specification, the book covers key topics such as:

- Genre
- Representation
- Audience
- News
- Comparative textual analysis
- Theoretical perspectives
- Crime fiction
- Passing exams

ISBN10: 0-415-34767-X (hbk)
ISBN10: 0-415-34768-8 (pbk)

ISBN13: 9-78-0-415-34767-9 (hbk)
ISBN13: 9-78-0-415-34768-6 (pbk)

Available at all good bookshops
For ordering and further information please visit:
www.routledge.com